REACHING
AMERICA

ISBN: 978-1-950791-87-3

Cover: TGS design team

Text layout design: Kristi Yoder

Printed in the USA

Published by:
TGS International
P.O. Box 355
Berlin, Ohio 44610 USA
Phone: 330.893.4828
Fax: 330.893.2305
www.tgsinternational.com

REACHING
AMERICA

Gary Miller

Table of Contents

Part One

THE DILEMMA

CHAPTER 1

Awake, Alive, and Multiplying!

The hot afternoon sun had finally penetrated the stone walls of the house, and soon her children would start trickling in for the evening. Leaning against the stone doorway, Orpah brushed a loose strand of hair from her eyes as she watched her children playing in the narrow street outside. Her husband Adriel had been gone from their home in Jerusalem for a few days now, and his absence always made time creep by. Adriel's business frequently took him to cities along the coast. Traveling in a caravan of fellow traders, Adriel took these trips to purchase products for his business.

The children always seemed more disagreeable without the authority of a father, and facing the constant quarrels alone was burdensome by the end of the day. Deciding it was time for a reprieve from housework,

Orpah picked up her water jar. The village well was the source of more than just water. It was where news was obtained and gossip was passed on, a place where their mundane toil could be briefly forgotten. Heading out the door, she almost collided with twelve-year-old Micah.

"Mother," he gasped wildly, "you can't guess what happened! That lame man—the one who always sits just outside the temple gate—you know which one. He was healed! He's walking around out there. Someone even saw him jumping."

Orpah set down her water jar. "Now slow down, Micah. You mean the beggar with the crippled foot? Walking? You must be mixed up. He's been sitting in front of the temple for years."

"Yes, that's the one!" Micah continued excitedly.

Slowly Orpah began to fit the pieces of this strange story together. This must be connected to that group of people who claimed the prophet Jesus of Nazareth had risen from the dead. Orpah's thoughts whirled. Could it be possible that even the resurrection story was true?

Her weariness forgotten, Orpah scurried down the narrow cobblestone street, hoping to learn more. She had heard about this man Jesus and the miracles He had done. But Jesus was now dead—unless you believed the story that He arose.

That evening as Orpah's family gathered for the evening meal, there was only one topic of conversation. Everyone had heard about the miraculous account, and each child wanted to share the details he or she had gleaned. One thing was certain: the story seemed true. Some had even witnessed the beggar's exuberant leaping as he praised God!

Orpah listened to the excited prattle of the children. What did all this mean? How could a couple of rough fishermen heal someone? One of the women at the well had said that according to her rabbi this new Jesus sect was attempting to destroy the Jewish religion. Frowning worriedly, Orpah wiped her hands on a towel and wished again that Adriel were home. He was a steady man, good at seeing through con artists and peddlers of erroneous doctrines. She was sure Adriel would be able to explain this latest fraud.

But the next day only brought more confusion. Word on the street was that the great Sanhedrin itself had gathered to consider the matter. Stepping to the door, Orpah could see clusters of women chattering excitedly. Obviously the religious leaders saw this movement as a dangerous threat to Judea's stability. Orpah turned to go back into her house, but not before she caught a glimpse of Deborah hurrying toward her.

Living next door, with children about the same ages, the two women saw each other often. Deborah had a reputation in the neighborhood of being cantankerous and troublesome. She was known as a woman to stay away from. It was common to hear Deborah's shrill voice echoing down the narrow cobblestone street, and though she was a close neighbor, Orpah didn't trust her and tried to maintain some distance. Today, however, a very different Deborah knocked on Orpah's door.

Orpah graciously invited Deborah in, silently bemoaning the mandatory hospitality that made it impossible to do otherwise. But an hour later, Orpah stared at the departing figure of her neighbor, trying to comprehend what had happened. Deborah had come to apologize for her past behavior. She had expressed regret for anger and lying. She had apologized for strife she had caused in the neighborhood. She had even confessed to stealing some flour from Orpah, something Orpah would never have known. And if this weren't enough, Deborah had also shared her newfound faith in this Jesus. With a countenance that glowed with peace and joy, she told of coming to believe in the resurrected Jesus and the change this belief had brought to her life.

Orpah sat in silence, trying to wrap her mind around this sudden transformation. Who were these mysterious, persuasive Jesus followers anyway?

Adriel returned home that evening, followed by a train of donkeys carrying his recent purchases. Orpah had never before been so glad to see him. Running out with shouts of joy, she and the children told

> ### Who were these mysterious, persuasive Jesus followers anyway?

of the tumultuous events that had occurred during his absence. Adriel listened, expressionless, as he and a servant unloaded the donkeys. When the work was completed, the family gathered for the evening meal, and the conversation continued to circle around the recent happenings. Two more priests had now joined the Jesus movement, and the whole city was in a stir.

Suddenly Orpah realized that Adriel had not been entering into the conversation. "Adriel, what do you think about all this? Do you think this movement is a threat to our people?"

Adriel paused thoughtfully before responding. "There have been many men who have risen up and created a stir among the people of Israel. But we Jews are a resilient people, and we have survived because our leaders have viewed such new movements with caution. But it's been a big day; let's clean things up and go to bed."

As she prepared for the night, Orpah marveled at Adriel's noncommittal reply. He was a man of strong convictions. Why this sudden reluctance to enter into the discussion?

After the children were asleep, and they lay in the silent darkness, Adriel suddenly spoke with quiet urgency. "Orpah, there's something different about this Jesus of Nazareth movement. It's not just the miracles. Some of those could be rumors and exaggeration, but I heard and saw some incredible things on this trip—things that are even more amazing than a lame beggar walking!"

Orpah waited breathlessly. One of the children stirred and Adriel waited, then continued in a quiet whisper.

"You know the men I travel with. They're good merchants; I have traveled with them for years. Every one of them has consistently pursued wealth and profit with passion. In the evenings we have always sat and discussed two things: how to increase business profitability and what we plan to do after we have made our fortune. It has always been that way."

Adriel paused. A donkey brayed in the distance, and Orpah waited.

"But this year something was different. Joses is the wealthiest in our group. He is the one we have always looked to for advice. A couple more trips and Joses won't have to work another day in his life. Well, at least he *wouldn't* have had to."

"What do you mean, Adriel?"

"Well, Joses recently became a Jesus follower, and last month he gave his land to that group. Imagine that. Year after year he has saved, scrimped, and traded. Now he suddenly gave it all away!" Adriel's voice rose and Orpah hushed him.

"But why? What will the group do with it?"

"That's what I asked him. And believe me, we had some long talks as we traveled. In the past, wealth was his primary pursuit. Now it's different. He believes that this Jesus was actually the Messiah who died for us. He said when a man grasps the beauty of Jesus' kingdom, earthly riches lose their appeal. It's a little confusing, but he said it's like a man discovering a pearl of such great value that he's willing to sell everything he has to buy it."

A soft breeze fluttered the curtain above them in the profound silence that followed. A dog barked in the distance.

"But that isn't all, Orpah. There is something else different about Joses. I could see it in the way he dealt with the merchants in Joppa and the concern he showed for each of us. In the past, nothing stood between Joses and potential profit. Now he is more cheerful and helpful. And amazingly, the same wealth he once craved he now views differently. It is almost like he sees wealth as a hindrance!" Again the silent darkness overtook them as each tried to grasp this mysterious change. Minutes passed, Adriel occasionally shifting, subconsciously hoping a new position would assist his inner wrestling.

"Adriel, are you still awake?"

"Yes."

"Wait till you hear about my conversation today with Deborah!"

All over Jerusalem, conversations like this were taking place during those first exciting days after Pentecost. People who had always been dogmatic, loyal Jews were suddenly sold-out, baptized followers of Jesus. As men and women believed in the power of the resurrected Jesus, they committed their lives to Him and to each other and lived totally different lives. Wealthy men sold their lands and relieved the anxieties of poor widows—and the world looked on in awe! The book of Acts says the church grew . . . daily! We read of newly baptized converts sharing their resources and eating together with "gladness and singleness of heart."[a] No wonder those first few chapters of Acts inspire us. The church was alive, awake, and growing rapidly!

This was not just an occasional convert, a misfit struggling to fit into the surrounding culture. This was transformation across social and economic lines. It included both men and women, both rich and poor, and was a beautiful picture of God's intent for the world. Person to person, house to house, the change was spectacular! In some ways it was like a highly contagious virus. One person was infected and his life was changed. He then came in contact with another person, and Christianity spread. It was evangelism the way we wish it were today. Even the religious and secular rulers sat up in alarm. Christianity was a powerful and conquering force to be reckoned with—and it was on the move!

---

[a] Acts 2:46

CHAPTER 2

What Is Different?

Those first exciting days of the early church must have been marvelous to behold. The end of the fourth chapter of Acts summarizes those exhilarating days like this:

> And the multitude of them that believed were of one heart and of one soul: neither said any of them that ought of the things which he possessed was his own; but they had all things common. And with great power gave the apostles witness of the resurrection of the Lord Jesus: and great grace was upon them all. Neither was there any among them that lacked: for as many as were possessors of lands or houses sold them, and brought the prices of the things

that were sold, and laid them down at the apostles' feet: and distribution was made unto every man according as he had need.[a]

So far in Acts, we don't read of any selfishness or covetousness. Instead, we read of selling, sharing, and serving. What a beautiful sight! We also don't read of problems or disagreements among that first group of believers. No wonder the early church multiplied and grew even in the midst of persecution. This wasn't just something that happened at a yearly revival—the church increased in numbers *daily*.[b] This was a movement you would want to join. It was a winning team.

Then, in the very first verse of the fifth chapter, we find these words: "But a certain man named Ananias,"[c] and from there on we read of believers involved in lying,[d] murmuring against other believers,[e] even disagreeing so sharply they couldn't travel together.[f] There was conflict over who could be accepted in the group,[g] what was required to be a disciple of Jesus,[h] and whether certain leaders were qualified.[i] In fact, after the book of Acts, the majority of our New Testament is letters to churches dealing with problems and trying to hold things together. Regardless how beautiful its beginning, it seems the Christian church had a very short honeymoon. Looking back from our vantage point today, the history of Christianity is littered with disillusionment and conflict.

So how do we view that initial tantalizing picture we read about

---

[a] Acts 4:32-35

[b] Acts 2:47

[c] Acts 5:1

[d] Acts 5:3

[e] Acts 6:1

[f] Acts 15:39

[g] Acts 11:2-18

[h] Acts 15:1-31

[i] 1 Corinthians 1:10-16

in the first part of Acts? Was it just a brief experiment that failed? Something that worked great at first but is not replicable? These are questions many of us have struggled with. Why doesn't evangelism work like that where we live? Why don't our neighbors come knocking on our doors asking what the secret is to our inner joy and happiness? Why are churches closing in America? Why is the fastest growing segment in our Western culture those who don't profess any religious belief at all?

To answer these questions, it is essential to briefly back away from our American experience. The Gospel of Jesus Christ is intended for the entire world, yet so often we become Western-centric in our thinking and blinded to global reality. God is at work in other countries and cultures as well, and looking over the wall into other settings may help us answer these questions. It may also assist us in reaching out here in America.

My first direct exposure to church life in a restricted country was in 2007. I traveled with another man to encourage underground Chinese church leaders, and the experience was eye-opening. I had read stories about the spiritual vibrancy of these "house churches." I had heard of their faithfulness during intense persecution and listened to accounts of strong leaders willing to stand against a godless communist regime. I was prepared to meet spiritual giants. What I found was not what I expected.

Instead of experienced leaders, I found leaders who were overtaxed yet undertaught. These men and women were strong on conviction but weak in experience. They were humble people who were well aware of their deficiencies. Tears were always at the surface, and earnest prayer was their constant companion. I remember sitting on my bed early one morning looking over notes I had prepared on the subject of prayer. I had an outline with bullet points, and thoughts I had gleaned from others in the past. But as I reviewed my notes, I kept hearing a group of pastors in the adjoining room. They had been praying for hours, starting before I was awake, and it seemed as if they would never finish. Yet it was not the length of time but their passion that moved me. I couldn't understand the language, but I could grasp the emotion. These people were praying in a way I never had. Putting my notes back in my briefcase, I realized there was no way I could speak to them about prayer. I was completely unqualified.

Some of them had been believers for only a few years, yet they had been asked to lead churches. One leader was only eighteen years old, yet was the primary overseer of several congregations. The church had grown so fast there simply was no one else in their city with more experience. Over and over I heard stories of healings, of miracles, of new believers. The expansion was happening faster than their ability to provide Bibles, so some churches had to share one Bible among the entire group. What I was seeing in China in 2007 was almost an exact replica of what we read about in the first chapters of Acts. In both scenarios, the church was expanding at an exponential rate, evidenced by miraculous events and purposeful, productive evangelism. How different from my experience in America!

Since that time I have had the opportunity to see this in other countries as well. I have seen Muslims—even a fervent Imam—come to faith. They had observed the incredible change in new Christians' lives and had come asking for the power of Jesus for themselves. Some of these were quiet citizens who became a powerful force in sharing the Gospel. Visions and miracles are not uncommon in these restricted countries, and reading their stories is every bit as exciting as the first chapters of Acts. There are so many similarities between the experiences of the early church and what is happening in places like China that there is no question in my mind—the book of Acts is not a record of a one-time event. It is a pattern of what real evangelism looks like. And it is still occurring around the world today. Then I look at America . . .

Why is our situation so different? Why don't we commonly see tremendous church growth, dramatic miracles, or radical life transformation stories? It is not for lack of programs. An incredible amount of money and energy has gone into advertisements, Gospel tracts, and all kinds of media intended to share the Gospel of Jesus Christ. Yet many of these efforts seem unfruitful. I know a sincere man who had a deep burden for the lost in his city. It had a population of over 200,000 people, and he was not sure how he could reach them. After spending time in prayer and talking to a few others, he came up with a plan—they would canvass the entire city.

Enlisting a group of men, they prayerfully went from house to house, covering the entire metropolitan area. At the conclusion they shared their results. Some people were friendly but uninterested; others slammed their doors in frustration. Only a few were interested in listening to their message. After all that well-intended effort, not one person committed his life to the Lord.

My goal in sharing this story is not to discourage this type of effort or to insinuate we should not pass out tracts. We should definitely have this kind of burden for the lost. But it does illustrate the dilemma we face in reaching out in America. Most of us have found that our culture is a difficult place to evangelize. But why?

CHAPTER 3

Does Anyone Really Care?

I n a 2018 study, 35 percent of Americans surveyed identified themselves as atheist, agnostic, or nothing in particular, up from 30 percent just three years earlier.[1] When only youth are polled, this percentage grows even higher. In the past few years this group, known as the "Nones," has caught the attention of many. What is causing this sudden surge of indifference toward religion? While many factors influence this, there is one piece of the puzzle we should not ignore: These are not individuals who were indoctrinated with a godless worldview as children and are now living out what they were taught. A majority, 78 percent, grew up in religious homes but later in life chose to abandon their parents' beliefs.[2] This is a shocking statistic. How did this occur?

Shifting Worldviews

For many of these, their worldview changed during college. Exposed to teachings that conflicted with their religious upbringing, they abandoned faith, finding answers in science and logic. Truth for them is in what is seen, not in the uncertain mystical realms of the invisible. These individuals, known as modernists, say they want facts and verifiable scientific proof. Since the existence of God can't be proved in the laboratory, they remain skeptical of miracles, supernatural explanations, or any unverifiable religious claims. Of course, many evolutionary claims are unverifiable as well, but the modernist remains convinced that science itself will eventually provide answers for questions of origin that are not yet demonstrable.

In the late 1900s, in reaction to the failures of modernism to produce utopia, another viewpoint arose that has been termed "postmodernism." For the postmodernist, truth itself is in question. In the halls of higher education, scholars are encouraged to question everything. They are suspicious of absolutes and ponder whether anyone can be certain of anything. Consequently, statements like "That may be true for you but not for me" are increasingly common. According to the postmodernist, each of us has the privilege of developing and embracing our own truth, and no one can say with certainty that anything is absolutely true. As illogical as this worldview may appear, its popularity is increasing, and we are seeing the results on many fronts. Of course, anyone who does not believe in absolutes will have little respect for the Word of God. Proclamations of judgment to come typically have little impact on an individual embracing a postmodern worldview.

Both modernism and postmodernism have had a huge effect on the receptiveness of the American public to the Gospel. Like a powerful vaccine, these worldviews have inoculated our culture, creating an inherent resistance to the Gospel. But this does not mean that people with a modern or postmodern worldview have lost all interest in spiritual things. They might think that is the case, but God is still working with them. He has placed a desire to worship in every human heart—a longing that is deep and not easily discarded.

Throughout history, people have tried unsuccessfully to satisfy this inner longing for God with other things. Augustine, a fifth-century theologian who had tried pleasure and various other distractions, finally concluded, "Our hearts are restless, until they can find rest in you." Blaise Pascal, centuries later, said there is a God-shaped vacuum in the heart of each man that cannot be satisfied by any created thing but only by God the Creator, made known through Jesus Christ.[3] Americans today have an abundance of things to cram into this inner hole, but they sense that something is still missing. They know their lives are not complete and are on a passionate pursuit for wholeness.

In 2019, David Zahl coined a new word in the title of his book *Seculosity.* Zahl argues that Americans, attempting to fill the void left by the abandonment of religion, are turning to all sorts of everyday activities to replace it. Careers, political involvement, technology, saving the environment, or even the perfect diet are pursued with passion and intensity, just as a devoted religious worshiper seeks after his god. "Our religion," he says, "is that which we rely on not just for meaning or hope but *enoughness.* "[4] Today we see people who are extremely passionate about the purity and perfection of the food they eat or the national park they hike in, but ignore the One who created it all.

Filling the Hole

The enabler of this cultural wave is affluence. We have the wealth to procure just about anything one could wish for, and possessions are a way for people to seek fulfillment. In fact, America is famous for overindulgence. Though America represents only 4 percent of the world's population, it consumes over 26 percent of its products![5] With an educational system promoting skepticism, a society awash in material goods, and a worldview that says present pleasure is all that really matters, it's no wonder we have a challenge.

Yet I think there is an even more seductive obstacle facing seekers today: electronic entertainment.

> With an educational system promoting skepticism, a society awash in material goods, and a worldview that says present pleasure is all that really matters, it's no wonder we have a challenge.

Electronic Pacifiers

One of the primary purposes of entertainment is to distract us from reality. Constant amusement diverts people away from God's call, even as it shapes their views and values. Pacifiers were never meant to provide nourishment. Rather, they just distract the child, sidetrack his concern, and offer a temporary placebo to divert him from his discomfort. Electronic devices do the same in our culture. When pain, loneliness, or any kind of anxiety rears its head, out comes the electronic pacifier. When serious thoughts about life or death threaten, the mind can be diverted by some funny video, movie, or online shopping, and reality is forgotten. Imagine how this can hinder the work of the Spirit in a person's life. The Lord begins to convict him of sin, but a few swipes on the electronic pacifier puts the focus somewhere else, away from the uncomfortable call of the Spirit. Few things dull spiritual desire like constant access to mind-numbing entertainment.

Describing the last days, the Apostle Paul predicted that "men shall be lovers of their own selves,"[a] describing this persistent pursuit after fun as "lovers of pleasures more than lovers of God."[b] Written almost 2,000 years before the electronic entertainment craze we are observing

---

[a] 2 Timothy 3:2

[b] 2 Timothy 3:4

today, Paul could not have written a more accurate description of our time.

Are Any Serious Seekers Left?

With a growing number of Americans checking out of religion and amusing themselves to death, why bother? How are Christians to compete with all this? How are we to interest someone in a quiet two-hour church service that calls the listener to make difficult, self-sacrificing choices? Is evangelism in America today an act of futility?

In 2006, Christian Aid Ministries launched a program called Billboard Evangelism. The goal was to place Gospel billboards along major highways throughout the United States. It was a bold approach. A phone number was provided, and volunteers prepared to answer calls from potential seekers responding to these Gospel messages. But would anyone actually call?

The answer is yes. In spite of all the affluence, distractions, and shifted worldviews, spiritual interest is still alive in America. As of 2019, the billboard program has received over 700,000 calls. While many of these callers just want to argue or share their displeasure with the sign's message, an estimated 30 percent are genuine seekers. There is obviously still a tremendous amount of spiritual interest. Why then do we see so little fruit?

CHAPTER 4

Do They Really Want What We Have?

Jesus warned His followers that the Gospel message would not be an easy sell. Describing the path, He warned that "strait is the gate, and narrow is the way, which leadeth unto life, and few there be that find it."[a] This is restrictive language, describing a path pursued only by serious seekers. Peter, a few years later, reiterated the narrowness and exclusivity of the Jesus way. "This is the stone which was set at nought of you builders, which is become the head of the corner. Neither is there salvation in any other: for there is none other name under heaven given among men, whereby we must be saved."[b] Peter says that Jesus

---

[a] Matthew 7:14

[b] Acts 4:11, 12

(no exceptions) is the only path to God. Given that the mantra for our age is tolerance, this message does not make our job of reaching out any easier.

The Irony of Tolerance

Our current culture exalts tolerance and despises exclusivity. "What right do you have," we are told, "to claim that your religious beliefs are superior to anyone else's?" But ironically, the tolerance being peddled isn't any less exclusive. D. A. Carson, in his book *The Intolerance of Tolerance,* notes there was a time in America when people had the right to believe what they wanted and even state it openly. Everyone's belief was truly tolerated. But today, the belief that all beliefs are of equal value is the only belief being tolerated. Carson says it like this: "Intolerance is no longer a refusal to allow contrary opinions to say their piece in public, but must be understood to be any questioning or contradicting the view that all opinions are equal in value, that all worldviews have worth, that all stances are equally valid."[6] The prevailing push toward "tolerance" is actually more restrictive and intolerant than the worldview it replaces. No longer does anyone have the right to believe that one opinion is superior to another. The only acceptable perspective is that all beliefs hold equal value.

"I am the way, the truth, and the life: no man cometh unto the Father, but by me."[c] There is no wiggle room in these words of Jesus. A "Christian worldview" does not attempt to force everyone to agree, but neither does it believe that all worldviews are of equal value. Therefore, this kind of "exclusive" position is deemed intolerant, and many turn away from the Gospel because it does not accept other religions. But intolerance isn't the only reason today's seeker might not be interested in what you have.

---

[c] John 14:6

The High Cost

Jesus was very clear. Not only did He teach that He is the only way,[d] but He said the cost of being His disciple is extremely high.[e] While that was obviously true in Jesus' day, it could be argued that the cost is even higher today. In our low-commitment culture, one of the burning questions we are almost fearful to ask seeking families is whether they are divorced. This is not a question we ask in our first encounter, but when we see children of varying ages we can't help but wonder.

If it does turn out to be a second marriage, the cost of following Jesus becomes very high. Choosing to separate from a spouse you love, knowing the devastating impact on the lives of your children, and questioning if this is actually God's will is an extremely difficult decision. For many, taking Jesus at His word comes at an incredible cost! Most of us have seen individuals come up against this and back away.

Others struggle with the concept of defenseless living. Jim[f] found the Lord early in life and became part of a local Protestant congregation. He married, had children, and came to believe that part of being a faithful Christian was physically protecting his family from harm. In fact, by the time he met someone who believed Jesus expected His teachings on nonresistance to be taken seriously, Jim had storage closets full of guns and ammunition. He was simply trying to be a good Christian father and protect his family. Today Jim has embraced defenseless living, but it was not easy.

Jim tells how difficult it was to believe that Jesus would want fathers to live in this violent world without lethal protection. It was unimaginable! Yet he kept going back to the actual words of Jesus, considering them, and eventually he embraced this basic teaching. Jim has been a faithful follower of Jesus now for many years, but he still remembers

---

[d] John 14:6

[e] Luke 14:33

[f] Names and details in stories throughout the book have been changed to protect identity.

how difficult it was to accept this truth. "I was convinced God wanted me to protect my family, and choosing to sell my guns and ammo was a huge decision." I can think of others who have come up against this "hard saying of Jesus" and walked away. This is one of the reasons seekers may not be interested in the Gospel you are presenting.

An Easier Path

Faced with the reality that Jesus' self-denying Gospel is a hard sell to a self-centered culture, churches have attempted to give Christianity a face-lift. While the old Gospel focused on taking up the cross and dying to selfish desires, the new alternative looks at people's desires and attempts to satisfy them. Whether it is popularity, wealth, acceptance, or just an entertaining Sunday morning experience, there is a church out there willing to help you achieve your goal. The Gospel Jesus brought was designed to transform the seeker to please God, but this new approach seems more focused on adjusting the holiness of God to fit the seeker. If churches are going to grow, it is argued, we must create an enjoyable experience that leaves the visitor wanting more.

Dr. Gary Gilley in his book *This Little Church Went to Market*, describes it like this.

> Growing churches are creating an atmosphere, an environment, of fun. So fun has replaced holiness as the church's goal. Having a good time has become the criterion of an excellent, growing church, since fun and entertainment is what consumers want. Yet Bible references encouraging churches to become havens of fun are, as one may suspect, lacking.[7]

Unquestionably, the message that God's primary goal is for you to be happy makes sharing the authentic Gospel of Jesus difficult. After all, if two paths lead to the same point, why choose the one that is more difficult? Why pick an unpopular counter-culture route if it is not necessary? That defies logic. So we, as followers of Jesus, have been given the task of sharing the uncomfortable truth that Jesus really did mean what He said. His message was clear. "So likewise, whosoever he be of you that forsaketh not all that he hath, he cannot be my disciple."[g] The Gospel of the kingdom of God has not changed. It still calls for total surrender, and this is another reason people may be slow to embrace what we have to share.

So, It's Just Them?

We have no control over some of these obstacles to evangelism. We cannot tell people that Jesus is just one of many ways to God, or redo our theology to make it more attractive. We do not have the privilege of making the path easier or softening the cross that God calls us to bear. Neither can we force people to become more interested in the Gospel. So, the thinking goes, if they don't want what I have, I might as well just focus on my business instead of my neighbor. If he ever gets serious about seeking God, he knows where I live.[h]

Do you ever find something like this drifting through your mind? There is something a little comforting about this line of thought. If the problem is simply a combination of American affluence, a love of pleasure, fascination with electronic entertainment, or a godless worldview, then I really can't do anything about it anyway, and it isn't my fault. Most of us have been tempted to subconsciously rest in this line of reasoning.

It's Not That Simple

But reality isn't quite that simple. Americans are not finding solutions for their inner cravings, and behind all the smiles there is an emptiness and a strong sense that something is missing. In spite of being

---

[g] Luke 14:33

[h] 1 Peter 3:15

constantly connected electronically, many are experiencing a sense of alienation and a need for relationship that is not being fulfilled. Consider the increase in the use of antidepressants. Between 1999 and 2014 there was a 64 percent increase in people using antidepressants, and in 2017 an estimated 16.5 percent, or one in six, non-Hispanic white Americans were using antidepressants.[8] Doctors prescribe antidepressants for more than one condition, but clearly the search is still on for a solution to anxiety and for lasting fulfillment and peace.

As Christians, we know where to find ultimate peace. We have experienced it. Not only inner spiritual peace for our hearts, but loving human relationships with others. Many of us have grown up in strong, loving church communities. When facing deep sorrow or disappointment, we have experienced an arm around our shoulders. We know what it is like to see a financial burden lifted, and we don't worry about being left alone when a family member dies. In short, we have exactly what people around us are searching for. So what is the problem? Why are we doing so poorly at conveying this reality to the lost?

Some of our congregations have the same last names as fifty years ago. Yes, taking care of our own families is important, but is that all God has in mind? Remember, every surname in your congregation was new at one time. So why aren't more people coming in?

CHAPTER 5

Do We Really Want Them?

I t was not supposed to be this way. David had led King Saul's men to victory in battle and enjoyed the thrill of returning home to the cheers of the admiring crowds. Besides, he knew God had specifically chosen him to be king. David had experienced God working through him in marvelous ways. Yet Saul had now turned against him, and he was in hiding. As David looked around that dim and dirty cave, he must have experienced major doubt. The Bible says he was captain of four hundred men, a puny match for Saul's military might. But perhaps most discouraging of all were the men David had attracted. "And every one that was in distress, and every one that was in debt, and every one that was discontented, gathered themselves unto him . . ."[a] This was hardly what David

---

[a] 1 Samuel 22:2

had visualized when Samuel had anointed him to be king.

We can imagine some thoughts that might have gone through his mind. *Surely I am meant for better things than this! How does God expect me to usher in a new day in Israel with this motley crew? Where are all the stable, well-adjusted, and contented men—the ones who consistently pay their bills on time and are good managers?*

The answer was simple. They were still back home, faithfully farming their land and minding their stores. Men who are content do not typically risk losing what they have to go search for something better. Maybe there is a lesson here for us today.

If you and your congregation have been actively attempting to reach out here in America, you already understand that seekers tend to come with difficulties, and they usually disrupt our normal, predictable way of life. They "intrude" into our well-scheduled, well-structured communities and ask awkward questions, bringing up topics we would rather not address. On Sunday we talk as if we want seekers, but many times when they appear, we find their presence inconvenient. At times, dealing with the consequences of their past infringes upon precious family time.

> On Sunday we talk as if we want seekers, but many times when they appear, we find their presence inconvenient.

Although the following categories are admittedly too simplistic, I am going to divide today's seekers into three basic types.

Manny Ishues

Let's call the first seeker Manny Ishues. He typically comes with a host of problems from his past. It might be financial challenges, marriage issues, or difficulty with interpersonal relationships. In short, Manny has many similarities to the men who sought out David in the cave of Adullam. But as he observes your structured lives, your nice homes, and your cars that always start, he knows he has found just what he has been looking for. To Manny, your church community looks like a well-oiled machine, so unlike the chaos in his past. Although he wonders if he could ever be totally accepted or actually belong, something within him craves what he sees.

Many of the Manny Ishues out there feel life has dealt them a rough hand. Like the men in David's cave, Manny comes hoping you will listen to him, walk with him, and help him find a better life. Manny has been subconsciously taught from his youth that others are to blame for his circumstances. He has grown up listening to stories about selfish landlords, lousy bosses, and wealthy people who oppress the common person. While you may have been taught that hard work is how people get ahead, Manny Ishues has learned that the only way to rise is to win the lottery, enroll in a good government program, or find a generous person (like you) to attach himself to. Remember, contented people do not usually go seeking, and depending on your zip code, you may find the majority of seekers are people like Manny Ishues. The time may come when you wonder why you ever opened the door when Manny first knocked!

Seekun Trooth

The second individual I want to introduce is Seekun Trooth. Seekun comes from a church down the road and is looking for more. He has found Jesus and has a powerful testimony. He is looking for doctrinal correctness and less hypocrisy, a church fellowship that is serious about following Jesus. Seekun loves his Bible and spends much time in prayer. He has tried multiple churches and found them wanting. He tends to be organized, serious, and intent on walking closer to God. Seekun Trooth is very different from Manny Issues. He is on a spiritual quest, and when he found you he was certain he had found what he was looking for: a group practicing the doctrines others have neglected, and likeminded people on a quest to be closer to God.

But before long Seekun Trooth begins to cause unrest. He spots inconsistencies in your congregation, and since he is serious about honesty and assumes you are too, he starts asking difficult questions. "Why are your people so serious about nonresistance but seem to have little interest in Jesus' teachings regarding the accumulation of wealth?" Or, "I like the fact that your sisters wear the head veiling, and that is partly why I am here, but why the disparaging remarks about churches like the one I came from? Even though they don't wear a veiling, they were the ones who cared enough to reach out to me."

In quiet moments, Seekun will question why he left his original church. He came hoping for more, but sometimes he is not sure he achieved his goal. While he appreciates the doctrinal correctness, he wonders about the apathy. Seekun Trooth came assuming he was joining a group on a spiritual quest to get closer to God. But sometimes it feels like your fellowship isn't actually on a journey. He gets a sense that you believe you have already arrived. And some of the questions he asks get really uncomfortable. Though you might not admit it, there are times you wonder why you picked up the phone when Seekun Trooth first called.

Indy Cided

The third individual you can't avoid in our culture is Indy Cided. Indy comes from a growing group of people who love to discuss all kinds of ideas, but are not quite ready to commit to any of them. Indy belongs to that group of people the sociologists call the Nones. She doesn't come with a Biblical foundation and may not understand the need for a worldview grounded in anything more than her own inner feelings. Neither does she see a need to reach conclusions during your discussion. But there's one thing Indy Cided will bring to your life—a host of questions!

Unhindered by a need to defend any one belief, Indy loves to throw out hard questions. She likes to speak of tolerance, of people's right to their own conclusion, and of the importance of not judging others. There is a good chance she is carrying wounds from a bad experience with a Christian. This person may have frustrated her by condescendingly providing simplistic answers to complex questions, hiding a lack of knowledge behind vague Christian clichés.

Debate will probably do little to persuade Indy, and an unwillingness to listen to her will simply hasten her down the path away from God. Gospel tracts attempting to convert her into a committed believer in three pages will have little impact and will likely cause additional harm. If Indy Cided is going to take a fresh look at Christianity, she will need to be exposed to disquieting evidence. She will need people with a humble spirit and a genuine interest in her life. She will need a person who is an unapologetic follower of Jesus Christ, someone who will remain a friend even if she chooses to remain unconverted. Indy has probably never met a Christian quite like that, and it will take many hours of listening and caring before she shows much interest in your beliefs. In fact, if your idea of evangelism is telling, selling, and compelling the lost to an immediate commitment to Christ, you will likely only do more damage to Indy Cided.

Do We Really Want Them?

This overview of potential seekers in America today is over-generalized, and as you interact with people, many will not fit exactly into any of these three categories. But if you have spent much time dialoguing with seekers, I suspect certain individuals came to mind as you read these summaries. And even though Manny Ishues, Seekun Trooth, and Indy Cided were different in many ways, all three had something in common: They came with baggage from their past.

My goal isn't to portray seekers in a negative light or to discourage you from reaching out. But we must be realistic. Jesus said, "No man can come to me, except the Father which hath sent me draw him."[b] God

---

[b] John 6:44

is actively calling, convicting, and drawing men to Himself. Our role is to care about the lost, and to individually and collectively demonstrate the character of God. We are to be praying for these people and preparing for the Lord to work.

Everyone Is Needed in the Field

Sometimes we don't see immediate results. After declaring that the fields are white and ready to harvest, Jesus said, "One soweth, and another reapeth. I sent you to reap that whereon ye bestowed no labour: other men laboured, and ye are entered into their labours."[c] Jesus is saying that those who are planting might not see the harvest, and the harvesters may not have been involved in the planting. But the point is this: Every follower of Jesus Christ should be involved in planting, harvesting, or both. And just because there isn't an immediate harvest does not mean it is time to stop planting. We won't always see results from our labor. But all of us are called to be working, and everyone is needed in the field.

It's Never Been Easy

Think back to the people who came to Jesus. It seems a high percentage were the poor, the down and out, and even individuals known to be immoral. There were exceptions, but many seemed to be people like Manny Ishues. Yet they felt safe coming to Jesus for help. Move on to the time of the apostles, and we see a similar pattern. Corinth was a wealthy city, but notice Paul's description of those who responded to the Gospel: "For ye see your calling, brethren, how that not many wise men after the flesh, not many mighty, not many noble, are called: but God hath chosen the foolish things of the world to confound the wise; and God hath chosen the weak things of the world to confound

---

[c] John 4:37, 38

the things which are mighty."[d] James seems to go further, insinuating that God is predisposed to the lower levels of society: "Hearken, my beloved brethren, Hath not God chosen the poor of this world rich in faith, and heirs of the kingdom which he hath promised to them that love him?"[e]

This is not to say that the rich and socially elite are excluded. But it does mean that we shouldn't be surprised if seekers come with problems. While some, like Nicodemus, were in the upper echelons of power, many of Jesus' most devoted followers were individuals living on the margins and came with deep issues. They came as military officers, greedy tax collectors, and immoral prostitutes. It was not usually the upstanding citizen, yet Jesus took time for them, and their lives were transformed by the Gospel. Today, there are stable, passionate, and gifted members in our congregations who originally came with major issues. Yet someone was willing to invest in their lives and help them find the ultimate source of healing.

The work is rarely easy. Manny Ishues may threaten to divide your congregation when members have differing opinions on how to respond. Indy Cided will probably ask difficult questions that you have never thought of and don't feel qualified to answer. Others, like Seekun Trooth, will reveal inconsistencies we may never have considered. He will make us realize we have more baggage of our own than we had thought. It takes a lot of humility to honestly confront our own hypocrisies and realize we have more to learn. But I encourage you to labor on. It won't be easy, but rest assured—when you reach out to the lost, you are laboring together with God. Remember, as it was in Jesus' day, so it is today: It is the sick who search for a physician.

---

[d] 1 Corinthians 1:26, 27

[e] James 2:5

CHAPTER 6

Evangelistic Obstacles

We love to read about great religious movements through-out history, and we look back on those times in awe—times when the church seemed vibrant and unstoppable. We like to read about the Reformation, when believers shared their faith despite severe persecution and churches grew exponentially, or the 1730s and 1740s, a time historians call the First Great Awakening. This movement started in England but soon spilled over into the New England States. Men like Jonathan Edwards, John and Charles Wesley, and George Whitefield preached powerful messages and wrote thousands of hymns. Multitudes testified that their lives were transformed. Later we read of Charles Finney preaching to thousands, and then of D. L. Moody starting in Chicago and traveling all over the United States preaching to millions of people. Regardless of what you think of their theology, there was clearly a strong hunger for the Gospel, and many people's lives were changed.

We read all this and cannot help but identify with King David. He looked back in his day and saw many amazing events in the past—times when God had responded in miraculous ways. But in times of discouragement he couldn't help but wonder why God wasn't moving like that now. "Our fathers trusted in thee: they trusted, and thou didst deliver them. They cried unto thee, and were delivered: they trusted in thee, and were not confounded. But I am a worm . . ."[a] I don't know if you have felt like this about evangelism in our day, but I have. At times I wonder why God doesn't seem to work here in America like He has in the past, or why it is so different than what we see in other countries.

> At times I wonder why God doesn't seem to work here in America like He has in the past, or why it is so different than what we see in other countries.

There are many ideas about why things are different in our setting. In this chapter we will look at some possible reasons why our situation is so different today. Then we will explore these obstacles further in the next chapters.

Cultural Obstacles

Talk to conservative youth who have a passion for evangelism, and it usually isn't long until the need to be a little more in sync with our culture pops up. "If we weren't so different, it would be easier to reach out. How can we reach out effectively while requiring converts to adopt major lifestyle changes that are hard to defend from the Bible?" Maybe this is an area we need to consider. After all, churches attempting to

---

[a] Psalm 22:4-6

live a counter-culture lifestyle are usually tenaciously holding onto a few remnants from their historical past that are difficult to defend from Scripture.

A similar dilemma confronted the early church. At the Jerusalem Council, we see a debate taking place regarding how much of the Jewish law a Gentile convert needed to embrace. These were men who saw value in many of the customs they had been raised with, and they did not want to lose it all. But there was also another fear. They did not want to trouble these new Gentile converts with details tied to their historical past if they were not required by God. After much debate, they sent out a letter explaining their conclusion about the issue, including their rationale for not requiring Gentile converts to adopt all the peculiarities from their own Jewish past. "For it seemed good to the Holy Ghost, and to us," they wrote, "to lay upon you no greater burden than these necessary things."[b] The apostles were obviously concerned that they not place unnecessary cultural requirements on new converts.

What is essential and what isn't? This is a question that churches throughout history have wrestled with, especially since the Industrial Revolution. The reality is, we don't all agree. We live in a fast-moving society, in a world that is constantly attempting to press us into its mold. Some things that at first glance seem completely unnecessary are actually an aid to maintaining a Christ-focused culture. Most of us have watched fellowships throw off customs and practices, believing them worthless and outdated, only to discover years later that they had lost more than they had gained. Removing some of these apparently superfluous specifics can feel liberating and helpful at the time. But a few years down the road, we realize that the detail we believed was unessential was actually a blessing.

Yet the truth remains. It is very possible for our churches to hang

---

[b] Acts 15:28

on to traditions that at one time held a purpose, but are no longer useful. Seekun Trooth will quickly identify these outdated practices, and a church that refuses to change simply because they "have always done it this way" will deter serious seekers. Determining what to discard and what to defend will require much prayer, open communication, and charity within a church. This can only transpire when there is strong confidence within a church that every member has a passionate desire both to maintain a counter-culture posture toward the world and at the same time lay no unnecessary burden on new seekers.

Ineffective Methods

Another possible reason our churches are struggling with outreach is that we are using ineffective methods. Sometimes the parable of the sower is used to teach that good sowers indiscriminately scatter seed and leave the results up to God. While it is true that increase is of God[c] and our job is to plant, this line of reasoning can be used to defend lazy evangelism. God does not intend that we sow arbitrarily,[d] and the primary lesson in the parable of the sower is not how to plant. The main lesson is how the Word of God should be received. We are to give thought to how and where we plant. That is simply part of being a good farmer!

In the book of Acts we see the disciples analyzing their effectiveness, talking about doors that were opening and discussing the impact of different ministries.[e] There were even times when they changed their methods or moved to another area due to lack of results.[f] They were

---

[c] 1 Corinthians 3:6-9

[d] In the Sermon on the Mount, Jesus said, "Give not that which is holy unto the dogs, neither cast ye your pearls before swine, lest they trample them under their feet, and turn again and rend you" (Matthew 7:6). We want to be careful about concluding that a seeker is a swine, but this verse seems to teach that it is wrong to offer something very valuable to someone who is unable to appreciate its value. This seems to teach that thought should be given before sharing with someone, and repeatedly sharing the Gospel with someone who continually scoffs and ridicules Christ is not wise.

[e] Acts 14:27; 15:4, 12

[f] Acts 13:46; 19:9

faithfully sowing wherever they went, but they were also considering the soil into which they were dropping their seeds. They had a strong desire not just to sow, but to be effective. They were also willing to make changes, not to the message, but to their approach.

I have noticed it is easier for us to start programs than to discontinue them when they aren't making the best use of our resources. Maybe it is the children's club that was started years ago but has no visible fruit. Or it is the yearly tent meeting, an approach that was useful fifty years ago when neighbors typically attended these public events and lives were changed. But now you look around at a revival tent meeting and suddenly realize that the only ones coming are your own people. The only reason you are still putting this tent up every year is because it was effective years ago. Maybe you have a prison ministry that seems to have little impact beyond providing bored inmates a brief diversion, but no one would think of stopping it. After all, it is our job to plant, and we shouldn't care about results.

Make no mistake. God can use these attempts in ways that are not visible to us, and just because we are not seeing immediate results does not mean we should abruptly stop. But we should prayerfully consider whether this is the best use of our time and energy. Our churches have limited human resources, and when we say yes to any endeavor we are saying no to another. We need to stop periodically and prayerfully consider each endeavor. Is this where God wants us to use His resources? Are there better approaches we should consider? It is very possible to be involved for wrong reasons. If all we are doing is wanting to feel good because we "did outreach," regardless of the approach, we are operating from wrong motives. It is possible that part of the reason your congregation is seeing so few results is because you are using ineffective methods.

An Arrogant Attitude

Recently I was asked to give a presentation called "Why No Converts from Our Community?" In preparation, I interviewed a number of individuals who are part of an Anabaptist church today but were not raised in an Anabaptist home. I wanted to know what kind of obstacles they faced in making this change.

Some challenges were what I anticipated, such as the struggle to accept nonresistance or fearing what their family might say at the next reunion about their change in appearance. But others took me by surprise. One sister mentioned not knowing how to host dinner guests. It was not something they had ever done, so the learning curve was steep. How much food do you purchase, and how do you plan such a large meal? Another spoke of the shallow conversation. They longed for the deep discussions they had in the evangelical church they came from. One said, "I have been in this church now for fifteen years, and during that time no one has talked to me about a personal struggle." Still another described a people group who are obsessed with food: "They call it hospitality, but I call it gluttony."

These were people like Seekun Trooth who love the theology and intend to remain with their particular Anabaptist group. But integration hasn't been easy. As I concluded my interviews, trying to categorize the input received, I realized that one particular obstacle was universal—a condescending or arrogant attitude. Some mentioned a lack of knowledge, or even interest, in other fellowships, but the predominant difficulty I heard regarding their Anabaptist group was an unwillingness to seriously consider another perspective. They had come assuming that this new biblically-oriented group of believers was as interested as they were in continuing to learn.

The people I interviewed were committed to remaining faithful. They were not disgruntled people who were shouting insults on their way out the door. I wonder if we could have the humility to learn from their observations. There are several reasons we should be listening.

First, followers of Jesus will be a teachable people. They want to know if they are in error personally or collectively. We should want hypocrisy exposed in our lives and congregations. Second, just how attractive will conceited people be to a seeker? How much impact will we have on our world if we are known to lack interest in others, are unwilling to consider our own inconsistencies, or are perceived (whether accurately or not) as condescending and arrogant? How will people see Jesus in a group that lacks humility?

Little Concern for the Lost

The last charge that is frequently levied, usually from men like Seekun Trooth, is that we no longer have a burden for the lost. He reads our history and reminds us that it has not always been this way. There were times in history when we carried God's passion for the lost. But now we are more concerned with our farms, businesses, and bank accounts than with the hell-bound neighbor next door. If we really cared, Seekun Trooth may say, we would be out on the streets, actively engaged in telling others about Christ. References are made to the example of the early church, and verses are quoted that describe their evangelistic zeal. After the initial persecution, those first believers "went everywhere preaching the word."[g] Their own safety forgotten, they had a passionate desire that everyone they met become acquainted with the kingdom of Jesus Christ!

During the Reformation, unspeakable torture was inflicted upon many of our Anabaptist forefathers, yet they were willing to risk sharing the Gospel with anyone who would listen. We hold them up as examples, yet our modern lives hold little actual resemblance. "If you would start telling people what you believe," Seekun Trooth will say, "you would be persecuted as well!" In other words, the peace we are enjoying is simply because we have become the quiet in the land. But is this true?

I don't think any of us would disagree that we need spiritual revival

---

[g] Acts 8:4

and a stronger burden for the lost. Perhaps our lack of zeal is part of the reason God is not moving as we would like. But there is another reason America is a difficult place to work. In the next section, let's take a fresh look at both our culture and at some of the methods we use.

Part Two

TAKING A
FRESH LOOK

CHAPTER 7

Searching for the Door

The Sawi tribe of western New Guinea, Indonesia, was well known around the world to be cannibalistic headhunters. When Canadians Don and Carol Richardson, along with their seven-month-old daughter, moved there in 1962, they knew it would be a challenging place to share the Gospel. But they didn't understand just how difficult. Almost completely isolated from the modern world, they faced malaria, dysentery, and hepatitis, in addition to the ever-present threat of violence. Don set about learning the Sawi language and understanding their culture, and was eventually able to share the message of Jesus to this remote tribe. It was at this point that he discovered he was even less prepared to evangelize these people than he had thought.

Famous for treachery and deceit, one of the Sawi tribe's tactics was to befriend surrounding tribesmen, invite them to a feast to fatten them up and gain their trust, and then kill and eat the unsuspecting visitor. When they were told the story of Jesus, a murmur of admiration swept through the Sawi listeners. Don Richardson praised God; the tribesmen were obviously being impacted by the Gospel message! But imagine his dismay when he discovered they were seeing this account through the lens of their culture and totally missing the message. In their view, it was not the faithful man whom they held in high esteem, but the most deceitful and crafty. The Sawis were admiring not Jesus, but Judas! Obviously, the traditional method of presenting the Gospel was not working. Don Richardson would need a different approach, a way that connected with their worldview. He eventually found it via a redemptive analogy they understood well.

Tribal warfare was normal among the Sawi people of New Guinea and surrounding tribes. Communities were decimated because of the intense fighting, yet eventually both parties realized that continued conflict was counterproductive and the war must end. However, valiant warriors had been killed and feelings were running high, so a lasting truce was not easy to procure.

It was out of this dilemma that a solution had emerged. One of the tribes would make the first move, offering the chief's own son to the other chief. If the other chief agreed, he would also offer his son. The exchange was then made, and each of these boys became known as a "peace child." Through them, reconciliation was possible between the warring factions.

Don Richardson, seeing the potential analogy in this ancient custom, used this to illustrate the truth of the Gospel, and suddenly the Sawis began to see the sacrifice of Jesus in a new light. They could grasp the pain of the Father, the need for Jesus as a sacrifice, and the blessing of restoration and peace. In his book *Peace Child*,[9] Don Richardson tells how the Sawi people began to listen to the Gospel message in a different way. He had found a way to connect on their level and was able to penetrate their worldview. He had found a way to guide them toward the door.

Finding the Door

Jesus is clear when using His sheepfold analogy that He alone is the true door. "I am the door: by me if any man enter in, he shall be saved, and shall go in and out, and find pasture."[a] Jesus alone provides access to the Father, and as Peter would say later, "There is none other name under heaven given among men, whereby we must be saved."[b] All of us must find that door! Over time, societies tend to build multiple cultural walls that must be navigated to find Jesus. In the Sawi tribe, it was their admiration of deceit that had to be circumvented. A pathway had to be found through their own knowledge, experience, and worldview to enable them to comprehend the Gospel message. This is true for all of us, but it may be more difficult in some cultures.

> Over time, societies tend to build multiple cultural walls that must be navigated to find Jesus.

I regularly hear people insinuate that there is just one way evangelism should occur. Citing the early believers in Acts, they state that any format other than telling the lost of their sin, sharing what Jesus has accomplished through His death and resurrection, and then calling people to repentance is a deviation from God's design. They argue that our job is simply to warn people of coming judgment, and leave the rest up to God. But I would ask that they go back and take a closer look at Acts. I find the apostles to be extremely creative in presenting the Gospel. They obviously were considering their audience and tailoring their message to connect with the listeners. Their message never altered, yet they were innovative in their presentation.

---

[a] John 10:9

[b] Acts 4:12

"Repent and Be Baptized"

On the day of Pentecost we read of Peter standing up and openly declaring, "Repent, and be baptized every one of you in the name of Jesus Christ for the remission of sins, and ye shall receive the gift of the Holy Ghost. For the promise is unto you, and to your children, and to all that are afar off, even as many as the Lord our God shall call."[c] It was a bold, understandable call and one that produced immediate results. About three thousand souls were added to the church in one day! But who were these people who repented? What kind of worldview did they have?

The people were Jewish. They knew there was only one God. They understood His law, and lived in fear of offending Him. In short, Peter's message was not difficult for them to comprehend. Many chose not to believe, but not because they didn't understand. Peter was clear, and he didn't need to spend any time clearing away debris. When Peter concluded his sermon, the door was right before them.

"Your Own Poets Have Said . . ."

Contrast Peter's approach with the creativity exhibited by Paul on Mars Hill. He observed their superstitions, commented on their devotion, and then launched his message by referring to an unknown god and a pagan altar he had seen along the road. From that unlikely beginning, Paul pushed against the Athenians' polytheistic assumptions and began telling them about a God who created the world and sustains everything. This must have been an astounding message to those pagans, something completely outside their box. He continued, citing one of their own heathen prophets and using pagan logic to help them see a God who couldn't be likened "unto gold, or silver, or stone, graven by art and man's device."[d] Amazing! This would be like witnessing to a Latter Day Saint and working in a quote from Joseph Smith's

---

[c] Acts 2:38, 39

[d] Acts 17:29

CHAPTER 8

Identifying the Soil

Craig stashed his backpack into the overhead compartment and eased himself into seat 13C. At least he had an aisle seat for the long flight ahead. As a believer in Jesus, Craig always made a point to introduce himself and learn something about his fellow travelers. He had a strong desire to reach out, so he always tried to find a way to connect with each person he met.

The young man in 13B, Stu Dint, seemed friendly, and before long a conversation was underway. Stu was on his way home from college for the summer. He described his life in school, mentioned some of the courses he was taking, and then saw the Bible Craig had slipped into the seat pocket.

"Hey, I noticed you have a Bible. That's really cool! You like reading it?"

"Yes, I do. Are you a Christian too?"

Stu cheerfully responded with a friendly smile. "No, I don't know much about religious stuff. Never got too involved. But if it works for you, that's awesome! I'm always excited when people find something that connects for them!"

Arriving a little early for his job interview, Craig glanced around the waiting area. He really needed this job. He had spent time praying but wondered if he even had a shot at it. Finally he was ushered into the office of Buzz Ness, the owner of the firm. Buzz listened to Craig's job history and was pleased with what he was hearing.

"So, Craig, you seem well qualified for the job. Are you open to working occasionally on weekends?"

"Well, I'd be open to working occasionally on Saturday. But not Sunday. I am a Christian, and the Lord's Day is important to me."

Buzz's eyebrows rose perceptively. "So you're religious. My wife always goes to church on Sunday, and occasionally I go with her. In college I became convinced that solutions are found in science, and that science will eventually provide answers for all our lingering questions. But I have seen a big change in my wife since she became a Christian."

Buzz paused and looked out the window. "It does seem like there is some force out there, some ultimate cause. But I'm just not convinced yet that Jesus is that force."

It was a beautiful Saturday afternoon in the park, and the family was enjoying some exercise, sunshine, and time together. Craig was playing Frisbee with his oldest daughter when a friendly young man suddenly interrupted them.

"Excuse me, sir. Would you have time for a couple questions?" Craig returned the Frisbee and told the visitor he would be glad to talk.

"My name is Evan Jellikal," the young man began as they both sat down on the grass, "and I was just wondering if you have a relationship with Jesus Christ. In other words, if you died tonight would you go to heaven or hell?"

As his family gathered around to listen, Craig and Evan began an enjoyable conversation. Evan, a divorced and remarried man, was currently on military leave and was using the time to go out and share the Gospel with others. He spoke of the challenges in the world, the great need for more people who are willing to share Jesus with others, and what a blessing it is to live in the United States.

"I tell you, Craig, I have seen a lot of violence over in the Middle East, and I am so glad God has blessed this country with a strong military. With the Lord's help, we are eventually going to eliminate those ungodly terrorists!"

Craig, a follower of Jesus in the hypothetical scenarios above, is faced with three different kinds of people. In each situation he would like to reach out and call them closer to the kingdom of God. But how? He wants to faithfully sow good seed in each encounter, but as a planter, what kind of soil is he dealing with? In this chapter we are going to look at two issues that are essential in identifying the type of soil. The first is the individual's worldview, or his relationship with truth. The second is his relationship with God and the words of Jesus. Let's start with truth.

Relationship with Truth

Absolute truth was something your grandfather assumed. He and his neighbor might not have agreed on what truth was, but they could definitely agree that it existed. But those days are over. No longer can we assume that individuals believe in absolute truth. And until you know how the person you are speaking to perceives "truth," you will struggle to make a meaningful connection. Stu Dint, in the first scenario, would

> **Absolute truth was something your grandfather assumed. But those days are over.**

be classified today as a relativist or a postmodernist. Truth to him is very fluid. A relativist sees all beliefs as equally valid, and not understanding this can cause you to assume you are making progress in a discussion. A relativist is fine with each individual having "a story," but he does not believe there is "A Story," or a universal narrative that applies to all.

Those of us growing up in Christian homes and being taught as children that the Bible is absolute truth have difficulty even understanding the Stu Dints of the world. But think about it like this: When an individual gets pulled into a movie or a video game, it tugs on his emotions and impacts his heartbeat. It seems amazingly real. Yet when he pauses to think, he knows he is engaged with something that is not authentic. It is just an illusion and will soon be over. This is how some postmodernists describe life. They hold out the possibility that the entire experience we are going through may actually be a mirage. Consequently, there are no absolutes and all beliefs are equal. Harold Pinter, a British writer and actor, describes life like this: "There are no hard distinctions between what is real and what is unreal, nor between what is true and what is false. A thing is not necessarily either true or false; it can be both true and false."[10] This is a postmodern perspective embraced by individuals like Stu Dint. You will need to understand this if you are going to reach out to him effectively.

Relationship with God

The second encounter Craig had was with Buzz Ness, an unbeliever like Stu Dint, yet with a completely different worldview. Buzz is convinced that truth exists, he just has not settled on the Bible as the source of it. In some ways, Buzz Ness is similar to the men in Athens in Acts 17. They believed there was a force out there, but had not come to a final conclusion as to what or who that force really was. So in the meantime they were willing to discuss the options, and Paul used this as an opportunity.

The chart below shows two continuums, and the difference between the audience in Acts 2 and Acts 17. Across the top is their level of interest. Vertically, along the side, is their knowledge of Jesus and their readiness to receive the Gospel. How we begin to reach out to an unbeliever is determined by where they are on these two continuums. We will return to this chart later.

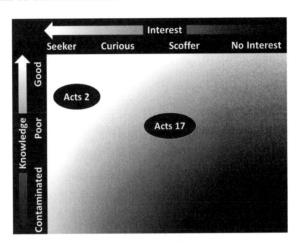

Relationship with Teachings of Jesus

Craig's third encounter was with Evan Jellikal, the young man who was eager to share the message of salvation to anyone who would listen. Evan firmly believed in absolute truth and that Jesus Christ is the Savior of the world. In some ways, he had a proper view of who Jesus is, and yet Craig was concerned that his understanding of the Gospels was incomplete. How could he help this man, who was obviously on fire for the Lord, get a better understanding of truth? Seed needs to be planted in each of these situations. Stu Dint, Buzz Ness, and Evan Jellikal all need guidance, but if Craig is going to be effective, he will need to give thought to the appropriate approach and customize his method to the need.

Examining Soil Conditions

In the parable of the sower, Jesus outlines four different types of soil.

Each received the seed, but the state of the soil had a huge impact on the yield. The first soil type was the wayside. This seed had barely stopped bouncing on the hard-packed soil before the birds came and devoured it. Most of us have worked with people like this. They show so little interest, it's hardly fair to call them seekers. The second soil was stony ground. These people are initially excited. This good news is exactly what they have been searching for! But just let them experience a little difficulty or stress in their relationship with Jesus or others, and they wilt.

The third type of soil looks more promising. We see good, rich soil ready to receive the Word, but unfortunately, time reveals that the Word of God was not the only seed residing there. A longing for wealth, a focus on business, or even just "a lust of other things"[a] begins to spring up like thorns. They may remain in the church, but there is little spiritual vitality or fruit in their lives. Finally, we see the fourth soil that Jesus called "good ground."[b] This is soil that is prepared and ready. Soil that allows the seed of God to have preeminence. And at harvest time the results are obvious!

This farmer didn't go out searching for bad soil or purposefully plant in soil that wasn't prepared. His goal was to sow on good ground. Yet as he tossed the seed, some did end up on the path and in areas that were not prepared. The same may happen in our lives as we reach out. When first meeting a potential seeker, the soil type is not always immediately apparent.

Centuries have passed since Jesus told this parable. Outwardly, we live in a completely different culture. But when reaching out in America, you will still observe these four basic types of soil. However, I suggest that we are facing another situation that makes sowing seed even more difficult. In one way it can be classified under the wayside soil, and yet it is a problem the early church didn't face. Maybe we could classify it as a different soil type. Let's call it contaminated soil.

---

[a] Mark 4:19

[b] Mark 4:8

CHAPTER 9

Contaminated Soil

We have a small family orchard, and a few years ago I noticed that one of our apple trees wasn't looking very healthy. I had planted six trees soon after purchasing our property, and initially all of them looked fine. For a few years everything looked good. We had nice growth, dark green leaves, and an abundance of apples at harvest time. (Unfortunately, a bit wormy.) Then one tree began to turn yellow and shrivel up. My investigation showed plenty of water, good soil with organic matter, and no weeds around the tree. There was no visible reason the tree shouldn't be thriving. Except for one factor. This apple tree was located close to a gravel driveway to which the previous owner had applied a soil sterilant. Some bushes planted close to this driveway had died as well, so I was certain I knew what the problem was—contaminated soil.

When soil is contaminated, your options are limited. Increasing fertilizer, adding mulch, or planting additional trees will not immediately mitigate the problem. Something needs to be done about the soil itself before trees will thrive or seeds will germinate. Unfortunately, we have a similar situation spiritually in America, which is one of the reasons it is so difficult to evangelize. In a very real sense, the soil in many seekers' hearts has become contaminated. They have observed the responses and the values exhibited in the lives of those who profess to follow the Lord Jesus and assume they understand Christianity. But sadly, many have never observed a good representation of Christianity. Let me share an example from our community.

Sherry's Soil

Sherry is a single mom who lives in our neighborhood. Abused as a child, she has always found it hard to trust men. It didn't help when her husband found more enjoyment playing video games than paying attention to his family. One day he ran off with another woman, who happened to be her best friend. Now Sherry was left with three children, an even greater suspicion of men, and no interest in a God who would allow this to happen.

Meanwhile, her divorced husband and his new wife "found the Lord," and began sending her information and tracts in an attempt to convert her to Christianity. Imagine what this did to her picture of God. While she was struggling emotionally, trying to survive economically, and raising her husband's children, he was promoting "Jesus" and the importance of "getting saved."

Place yourself in her position for a moment. You are walking down the street and some bright-eyed young man hands you a tract telling how much God loves you. What would go through your mind? If you had experienced Sherry's life, what would the word *Christianity* mean to you? Sherry has contaminated soil. Telling her that God has a plan for her life, that Jesus loves her, and that He is in control of everything that happens in her life rings hollow. Germination is unlikely.

Sherry has spent a good deal of time in our home and with others in our church community. We have read from the Bible, tried to listen to her pain, and spent time in prayer with her. But the bottom line is this: She still can't visualize God as a loving Father. We still have hope for Sherry and haven't stopped praying for her. But we are well aware that we are dealing with polluted soil.

Widespread Misrepresentation

I wish I could say that Sherry is a rare case, but she isn't. The person you meet on the street may have been abused by clergy, been taken advantage of by a ruthless "Christian" businessman, or been turned off by some disgraceful religious hypocrisy.[a] It seems we are living in the middle of a multitude of painful stories. The news media seems to enjoy publishing the latest religious scandal. News reports outlining the titillating details of sexual abuse or financial corruption in the church have become a frequent occurrence. People are continually bombarded with religious hypocrisy.

In addition, consider how the American people perceive the average evangelical Christian. Recently a poll was taken asking Americans whether refugees should be welcomed into the country. For a follower of Jesus, this should not be a difficult question. Anyone having even a cursory understanding of His teachings should know how Jesus would respond. He gave clear commands that we are to befriend "the poor, the maimed, the lame, the blind,"[b] and I can't think of a better way to describe many of these landless, homeless, helpless people. America is extremely wealthy and possesses tremendous ability to help those in

---

[a] It has been said that behind every atheist is a wounded theist. They have been injured in some way by a person professing to be a Christian, and this has caused them to doubt the existence of God.

[b] Luke 14:13

need. What an amazing opportunity! But refugee camps are bulging. The current refugee crisis is overwhelming governments and organizations who are attempting to help. One would assume that American Christians would be first in line to assist these traumatized people.

That is why the results of this poll were shocking! Only 25 percent of white evangelicals believed the United States has a responsibility to these refugees. In contrast, 65 percent of religiously unaffiliated citizens felt that the U.S. has a responsibility.[11] These statistics should shock us. This means that the person who does not believe in Jesus is more than twice as likely to reach out to a foreign refugee as the one who professes to follow Him! Even the *New York Times* noticed this hypocrisy, printing this observation in an article titled "Why People Hate Religion." The article included the following: "In one of the most explicit passages of the New Testament, Christ says people will be judged by how they treat the hungry, the poor, the least among us. And yet, only 25 percent of white evangelicals say their country has some responsibility to take in refugees."[12]

No wonder the average seeker in America is confused and disinterested in Christianity!

Global Confusion

America is known worldwide for its military might. In 2019, the United States spent far more on its military than any other country in the world. In fact, if you combine the defense spending of the next six countries with large military budgets, the United States spent *forty billion* more.[13] That is an incredible amount of focus and spending on defense! Since America is perceived around the world as a "Christian" nation, most people believe this is consistent with Christianity. Even more disturbing, the average white evangelical Christian is a proponent of increasing military spending.

One could assume Jesus had never opened His mouth about turning the other cheek,[c] loving your enemies, or doing good to them that hate

---

[c] Matthew 5:39

you.[d] By observing the words and actions of the modern evangelical church, a seeker would never know that the early Christians refused to take part in warfare or that many throughout church history have died rather than defend themselves.

This issue is huge, since the message of loving your enemies was a pivotal and revolutionary principle in Jesus' teachings. He did not teach us that we should love other people only as long as it is easy. His life and death clearly demonstrated what He meant by His teachings. American church-goers regularly hear of the life of Jesus, of His unjust death, and even of His final request that His persecutors be forgiven for their heinous crime. But somehow the idea that this is to be replicated in the lives of His followers has been forgotten. American Evangelicals today are not known for nonresistance. Consequently, the average unbeliever in America has a warped view of what Christianity is. Like soil polluted by harsh chemicals, millions of minds have been contaminated against the God of the Bible, often by the very ones who claim to be His representatives.

> American churchgoers regularly hear of the life of Jesus. But somehow the idea that this is to be replicated in the lives of His followers has been forgotten.

Reaching the Nones

In the last chapter we looked at the difference between Peter's audience in Acts 2 and the men Paul preached to in Athens in Acts 17. The presentation of the Gospel was entirely different based on their knowledge and level of interest. Yet in America it is even more challenging when we consider the group we mentioned earlier, the Nones.

As different as the two groups of listeners were in Acts, they did have

---

[d] Matthew 5:44

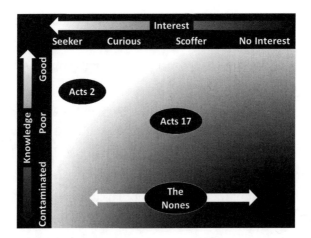

one thing in common: With regard to Jesus, they were likely both starting with a blank slate. They didn't have a preconceived idea of what
Christianity looked like, and those early teachers were able to start with
the basics and build.[e] And in some ways this describes the Nones. Like
the men of Athens, they like to posit ideas and theorize all manner of
possibilities but avoid a final conclusion. Yet in another way they are
very different. Unlike those men on Mars Hill, the Nones have already
considered Christianity, seen the inconsistencies and hypocrisies, and
drawn conclusions from their observations.

So how do we reach out to people who have a preexisting yet
improper view of Christianity? Ongoing debate may only further convince them that Christians are narrow-minded and unwilling to see the
issue from their perspective. So what are we to do?

---

[e] In a book about G. K. Chesterton, Emile Cammaerts wrote, "When men choose not to believe in God, they do not thereafter believe in nothing, they then become capable of believing
in anything."

CHAPTER 10

What Would It Take?

I have lived across the street from Carlos for about nine years. Carlos is a diligent, hardworking Hispanic man, and he and his wife make very good neighbors. Both of them worked for many years and now they are retired, so they have plenty of time for trips, cruises, and working around the house on various projects. The first Christmas after we moved here, my wife made pastries for the neighbors. I knocked on Carlos's door, and I could tell this was a new thing. He thanked me profusely, and a few days later our doorbell rang. There stood Carlos with a big smile and plate of tamales. This tradition has continued ever since. I stop in with some Christmas baked goods, and it is not long until Carlos arrives with a fresh batch of tamales. We chat occasionally when we pass by on walks and help each other out with small needs. We have a good neighborly relationship.

A few years after we started this Christmas exchange, I dropped off my wife's pastries, but somehow Carlos forgot the tamales. A week or so later a group of youth from our church went around the neighborhood singing Christmas carols, and they stopped at Carlos's house. Their presence reminded him of his neglect, and while they were still singing at the front door he ran out the back and across the street to our house. There he stood with a plate of tamales while the youth continued singing to his wife. Carlos likes to keep things even!

Carlos grew up going to church, but when he was nineteen years old he observed hypocrisy in the leadership and left. He has never been back. We have talked about his experience, and Carlos says he believes in God, but not religion. In addition to hypocrisy, Carlos has been turned off by assertive and aggressive religious proselyting. He has had people come to his door, trying to convince him to join their group, and this has pushed him even further from the truth. One evangelistic outreach team kept arguing with him, not leaving until he threatened to call the police. All this has impacted Carlos's perspective of Christianity. So he spends his time vacationing, watching television, and maintaining and improving his landscaping. With regard to religion, Carlos has checked out.

Connecting with Carlos

What will it take for Carlos to take another look at Christianity? It has

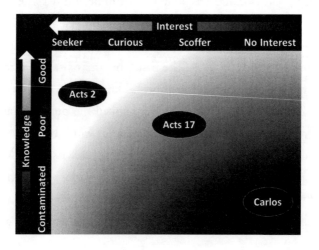

been over forty years since he left his church, and his view of Christianity has definitely been contaminated. In addition, over the years he has lost interest in even thinking about God. Carlos and his wife have attempted to fill that inner void (intended for God) with vacations and pleasure. Now they are getting older, and as their bodies wear out, even the Caribbean cruises have lost their charm. He comes back complaining about lousy service, the price of beer, and the difficulty in getting rooms with a balcony. Recently he was able to get a room with a balcony overlooking the ocean, but when he arrived, the balcony was so small there was barely room for one chair. Carlos is having difficulty finding fulfillment. But how can I plant when the seedbed is polluted and there seems to be little interest? What would it take for Carlos to question his perspective and actually adopt a different worldview?

Adopting a New Worldview

We don't change worldviews easily. To illustrate, consider what it would take to change yours. I will assume you believe that God created our world. You have believed this for many years, and consequently, the theory of evolution seems unreasonable. (A little like Christianity does to Carlos.) How could I persuade you to rethink this position? If you were given a tract titled *Evolution Is the Answer,* is there anything that tract could say that would convince you that our world evolved? Probably not. Your belief is thoroughly entrenched and embedded in your worldview. You have observed many things over the years that have further solidified your belief, and daily observations continue to reinforce your certainty that creation is the only reasonable viewpoint. So what would it take to move you from a confident creationist all the way to a confident evolutionist?

Exposure

You would first need to be exposed to some new facts, something you have not seen so far. It might be some new links in the evolutionary chain, or maybe some new evidence that causes you to doubt the veracity of the Biblical creation account. This would not be easy! In fact, you would probably need multiple exposures to evidence that conflicts with your present belief. But let's assume that this occurred. This alone probably would not be enough. You would need to thoroughly examine these facts that are challenging your belief in creation.

Investigation

If I read or hear something that conflicts with my opinion, my tendency is to either dismiss it outright or do some investigation. Facts that conflict with our worldview are disquieting. Something within drives us to

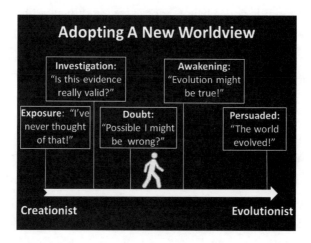

disprove the evidence. But let's just assume that all the facts regarding the truth of evolution line up. While this might shake your faith, you probably would not say anything to your friends at church. You have been shaken, but you are not ready to reveal your uncertainty. Again, this would take time. Depending on your personality, you might mull over these new facts for a long time, maybe months or even years. But assuming the evidence kept accumulating, and your investigation kept affirming these facts, eventually you would begin to entertain some doubt.

Doubt

Now you are considering the possibility that your current worldview is resting on inaccurate data. You would still be very reluctant to say anything to friends. After all, you have not concluded anything, and voicing doubts might affect your social life. But if the evidence kept lining up, and you were determined to be intellectually honest, you would have no recourse but to doubt your belief in creation. You have not yet abandoned your position, but you are caught between two opposing beliefs.

Awakening

Finally, there would be an emerging realization that in spite of your previously stated belief, it is possible that evolution might be true after all. Instead of just looking back at what you believed, you are starting to look forward. Maybe, you decide, evolution is true after all! At this point you might be willing to mention your inner ponderings to a few close friends, but this is risky. How would your closest friends respond if you told them you were suspecting evolution might be true? (Probably about like Carlos's friends if he informed them he was considering Christianity!)

Persuaded

Eventually, assuming no contradicting facts came out and you had sufficient passion for truth, you would come to believe in evolution. You would finally renounce your belief in creation and now believe that Charles Darwin was right. This is difficult for us to imagine, knowing there are major problems with the evolution theory. But don't miss the message: This is what we are asking our unbelieving neighbor to do. We are expecting him to look at a few facts we present and then gallop across this continuum. But regardless how valueless you esteem his point of view (he probably feels the same about yours), there are two basic realities we must come to grips with.

First, everyone you meet already has a worldview. They are seeing the world through a certain lens, and their perspective has developed over time and through many life experiences. Just as you cannot understand why they see the world as they do, they are probably just as convinced that your belief lacks supporting evidence. If we fail to understand this basic truth, we will have difficulty being effective in reaching out. So often our evangelistic methods appear to lean on the assumption that Christians are the only thinkers out there. Others just haven't been exposed to facts. So we approach people as if they were nonthinkers. We try to share the information they lack, and then we can't understand why they don't change. Which leads us to the second reality.

Even faced with irrefutable evidence, it is rare for us to quickly change our worldviews. Go back for a moment to the initial question. How good would a tract on evolution need to be for you to immediately change your opinion? The answer is simple. Regardless how airtight the arguments and facts presented, it would take more than a little time and information.

So What Will It Take?

Let's go back to my neighbor Carlos. He has over sixty years of life experiences to draw from. All of these support his current worldview. So what am I to do? What might cause him to revisit faith in God?

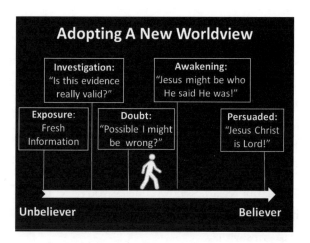

I would suggest this will look very similar to you accepting evolution. As the chart suggests, this will be a process. The process includes two additional powerful components we haven't discussed yet.

So far we have only considered visible factors that impact movement toward a faith-based worldview. But there is another reality we dare not neglect as we consider reaching out to the lost. The Holy Spirit will be encouraging movement along this continuum toward faith in God and Satan will be discouraging it. Jesus said, "No man can come to me, except the Father which hath sent me draw him."[a] Much more is going on than just the visible aspects of presenting the Gospel properly. Our efforts will be in vain unless the Spirit of God is involved.

Fervent Prayer

We are simply working with God, and ongoing prayer must precede, envelope, and overshadow all of our efforts. We so easily become enthralled with the visible, assuming that we are the primary agent in "bringing the Lord" to the lost. But remember, God was active in a person's life before you became involved. It is essential that you be connected *to* God if you are going to be effective in working *with* God. He can, and sometimes does, draw people to Himself without utilizing other humans. The conversion of the Apostle Paul is an example of this. But these occasions seem rare. For some reason, known only to God, He has chosen to incorporate stumbling, bumbling humans in His work of reconciliation, and continual fervent prayer must be central to our endeavors.

There are many ways we can be involved in sharing the message of the kingdom of God. Where obstacles to belief exist, those hindrances need to be removed. This is the purpose of apologetics.[b] The early church was surrounded by a heathen culture, and there was a great need for individuals to provide a reasoned argument or defense for Christianity. This is what Paul did at Athens, and we find many other early Christian writers like Origen, Tertullian, and Justin Martyr doing the same as time went on. They were working with people from pagan backgrounds. Our culture is

---

[a] John 6:44

[b] The word *apologetics* refers to the act of making a defense. Stephen, in Acts 7, was doing the work of an apologist. In the Christian faith, an apologist is one who attempts to remove obstacles to faith. He may point out inconsistencies in evolution or use history to defend the historical reliability of the Bible. While an evangelist proclaims the Gospel, an apologist attempts to remove obstacles to it.

rapidly moving in the same direction, and in many ways we are entering into a similar setting. Today it is very common to find agnostics like Stu Dint or Buzz Ness right next door.

There are also those who profess Christianity but whose lives bear little resemblance to the Jesus they profess to follow. This has always existed, and all of us are susceptible to hypocrisy. Yet in our day, this problem has grown to where it seems normal for individuals like Evan Jellikal to profess to be followers of Jesus without following all His teachings. Doctrines have been developed that allow a man to feel confident he is saved, while avoiding the daily cross that Jesus declared is required.[c] And, of course, all this has created the contaminated soil we are confronted with.

Disquieting Exposure!

Just as you would never consider changing your worldview without first being confronted with facts which shake your current set of beliefs, neither will my neighbor Carlos. He will need to be presented with an unsettling reality. But what exactly would this look like?

For Thomas it was seeing a risen Jesus. The idea of a man rising from the dead just did not fit into his worldview. But when he saw the wounds for himself, it shifted his entire belief system. For Saul of Tarsus, it was a bright light on the road to Damascus. He had believed Jesus was a hoax and His followers a threat. But coming face to face with Jesus Himself was the disquieting exposure Saul needed. He would never again be the same.

Looking back through history, we repeatedly see people coming face to face with disquieting exposure and having their worldview shaken. During the Reformation many turned to Jesus after watching faithful martyrs endure torture and willingly die horrible deaths rather than renounce their faith. That was enough to persuade many to take another look at this Jesus. In the next section we will consider some ways God is calling believers today to provide unsettling reality!

---

[c] Luke 14:27

Part Three

DISQUIETING EXPOSURE

CHAPTER 11

Christianity as a Vocation

O ur world desperately needs to see the life of Jesus Christ lived out in His followers. Seekers need proof that He actually has the power to change lives. They need to see churches, businesses, and homes that are radically different. But none of this can happen until individual followers understand the inherent calling upon their lives. Until our lives are surrendered, there will be no disquieting evidence. Part of our challenge is that we tend to regard serving the Lord and reaching out to others as a part-time endeavor, something we add on to our regular activities. We compartmentalize our lives, and evangelism becomes something we occasionally do rather than a way of life.

In 2018, Christian Aid Ministries' SALT Microfinance program launched a new program to reach out to lower income Americans. It is a twelve-week financial course called Salt and Light, and the goal is to provide Anabaptist churches with a method of developing and building relationships with their neighbors. The program, however was slow in taking off, and it didn't take long to realize there was a problem. And ironically, the primary problem is us. We normally have busy schedules, and working with hurting people takes time. People realized that effective outreach would impact their calendars and social schedules. Agreeing to reach out locally is not a part-time project, and we draw back from that commitment. For many of us, the cost is simply too high.

Committed to Our Calling

Paul told the church at Ephesus, "I therefore, the prisoner of the Lord, beseech you that ye walk worthy of the vocation wherewith ye are called."[a] This word *vocation* speaks of a heavenly occupation, an all-encompassing calling that affects every part of your life. This was how those first believers regarded following Jesus. It was a decision that cost everything and touched every part of their world. Today it is easy to slowly absorb the idea that Christianity is primarily a change in position. But becoming a new creature in Christ is not intended to just change a person's standing before a Holy God, it will also change how he lives before unholy men. Every part of his life will be transformed! It will change his passions, his perspectives, his purpose—everything. Until we grasp this foundational truth, we will have difficulty reaching America.

It is essential to understand that Christianity is a full-time vocation, not a part-time endeavor. When a

> But becoming a new creature in Christ is not intended to just change a person's standing before a Holy God, it will also change how he lives before unholy men.

---

[a] Ephesians 4:1

Christian refuses to relinquish control to God over every part of his life, he becomes one more "soil contaminator," confusing people and doing damage to the kingdom of God. So what does committing to Christ as a vocation look like? Consider how Jesus described the calling on His life.

Jesus' Motivation for Ministry

Jesus made some astounding statements about the driving motivation behind His ministry. Speaking to His disciples after talking to the woman at the well, Jesus said, "My meat is to do the will of him that sent me, and to finish His work."[b] What an interesting way to describe his ministry! His disciples had brought some food, but Jesus responded with this statement, seeming to say that He was drawing His life, enjoyment, and daily sustenance from doing His Father's will. Does this describe your life and ministry? Is the knowledge that you are faithfully serving God enough?

Jesus described His purpose several times, and there is a consistent theme in His words. "I seek not mine own will, but the will of the Father which hath sent me,"[c] and later on in His ministry: "For I came down from heaven, not to do my own will, but the will of him that sent me."[d] These are challenging declarations. They are strong statements that not only describe His motivation, but also provide a reference point to examine ours. As I watch church splits, infighting among religious leaders, and even conflict within missions, I cannot help but wonder. What is the underlying cause of continual conflict? Is it actually the result of believers committing to doing, as Jesus did, not their own will but the will of the Father? Or is it primarily the result of people within churches, missions, and even church leadership teams who are attempting to "serve

---

[b] John 4:34

[c] John 5:30

[d] John 6:38

the Lord" according to their own will?

Perhaps the most challenging words Jesus spoke regarding His ministry was this unequivocal statement: "I do always those things that please him."[e] That is a powerful declaration! These words encapsulate Jesus' entire life, not just the times we read of Him doing great things. He spent time eating, sleeping, and sharing daily life with those around Him. In fact, from what we can glean from the Gospel writings, the majority of His earthly life seems to have been spent at home, working in a carpentry shop. Yet He was able to confidently declare that everything He did pleased His Father! Wouldn't you have liked to observe His daily life? What if you could have sat in the corner of His shop unobserved and watched how He worked, or seen how He responded to that difficult customer? What might you have learned? But don't miss the lesson here. Jesus lived, in many ways, just like everyone else around Him. Yet the overriding purpose and vocational calling on His life was totally different. His goal was simply to please His Father. Ministry was not something He occasionally turned on and off. Obedience to His Father was a vocation, and it permeated every part of His life.

Observations from Jesus' Life

We have relatively few details about the life of Jesus, yet there is much we can glean. Those few years the Gospels focus on tell so much about His priorities, His passions, and the approaches He used in reaching out to people. It was so different from the prophets. When I read about the prophets, I don't get a warm, fuzzy picture. The Old Testament prophets seemed to be a sober sort. They were men whom God commanded to proclaim truth to people who had turned from it, and their message usually was not very pleasant.

Reading about temperamental Jonah, weeping Jeremiah, or even

---

[e] John 8:29

John the Baptist, who wore strange clothes and ate unusual food, I don't think of individuals I would enjoy sitting with and casually chatting about the day. These do not seem like men you would just hang out with. They were serious men who were calling the people to repentance and warning about judgment to come. And while Jesus also did this, we see Him holding children, interacting with the hated Romans, even being accused of gluttony, drinking wine, and befriending publicans and sinners. We certainly don't read these charges being leveled against men like John the Baptist!

Jesus seemed to relate well to a wide range of people, and this shook their presuppositions. He ate with sinners, but he did not sin with sinners. He engaged in normal earthly activities without being worldly. This was the paradox of Jesus' life.

Social status did not seem to faze Him. If anything, He seemed to prefer the poor. Yet some of His greatest admirers apparently were wealthy. It is difficult to categorize Jesus or His ministry. One of my favorite passages, one that reveals much about His approach to ministry, is in the book of Mark. It follows a tremendous amount of activity and emotional trauma. Jesus' cousin John had just been beheaded. Jesus and His disciples were tired, and He knew they needed a break. "And he said unto them, Come ye yourselves apart into a desert place, and rest a while: for there were many coming and going, and they had no leisure so much as to eat. And they departed into a desert place by ship privately."[f]

A Needed Break

Jesus and His disciples got tired just like we do. They were finally going to get a little well-deserved break. But the account says the people ran around to the other side of the lake, and when the disciples' little boat arrived, there were the masses of needy people again. I would have been

---

[f] Mark 6:31, 32

tempted to turn that boat around and head back out to sea! But notice how the writer describes Jesus' response: "And Jesus, when he came out, saw much people, and was moved with compassion toward them, because they were as sheep not having a shepherd: and he began to teach them many things."[g] There are several basic lessons in this account:

1. *The driving force in Jesus' life was to please His Father.* He saw these people not just from the perspective of a weary man who was overworked, but through the eyes of His Father.

2. *Before Jesus began to instruct and teach, He was moved with compassion.* Whatever the ministry, it is essential that we frequently revisit how we see those we are trying to reach. Is compassion our primary motivation in ministry? Or are other motives involved? It is possible to preach good sermons, counsel the confused, or alleviate poverty and yet have misguided motives. If I don't have genuine compassion and love for those I am ministering to, the Apostle Paul says it "profiteth me nothing."[h]

3. *Jesus did not ignore their basic physical needs.* Immediately following this passage, Jesus took the few provisions the people had and multiplied them to provide for their hunger. He didn't seem to draw any lines between physical and spiritual needs, and we shouldn't either. People were hungry and Jesus had compassion. And although we don't find Jesus continuing to feed these people day after day, He saw hunger, was concerned, and did what was in His power to mitigate the need.

4. *Humans are finite; they have physical and emotional limitations.* Sometimes we act as though God intends for us to be

---

[g] Mark 6:34

[h] 1 Corinthians 13:3

superhuman, and that every soul out there is our responsibility. Consequently, ministry means running breathlessly from one event to another, trying to accomplish things we were never designed to achieve. But God made us and understands our limitations. He knows that we are made from dust,[i] and we should never feel guilty about our human limitations. But neither should we use this as an excuse for apathy or lack of commitment. We have examples all through history of men and women who have accomplished amazing feats through the power of God!

Engagement and Withdrawal

God, from the very beginning, intended for life to have times of engagement and times of withdrawal. We see this when God created the world. He worked, He stopped and reviewed what He had created, and then He rested. We see this again in the Old Law. There were six days for work, and then a Sabbath for rest. There were specific times when the children of Israel were to plant and harvest. But there were also times of feasting, enjoying the fruits of their labors, and thanking God for His blessings. God built a certain rhythm into their lives that included times of labor and times of resting. We see this in the life of Jesus, and as His followers our lives should also have a healthy rhythm. But we must also remember that vacation was never intended to be our vocation. Rather, it is to prepare us for continued ministry.

Even though God is not calling us to a life of frenzied service, it is essential we never lose sight of our purpose. Jesus' mission was clear: "For the Son of Man is come to seek and to save that which was lost."[j] As Christians, we are called to follow in His steps.[k] Jesus participated

---

[i] Psalm 103:14

[j] Luke 19:10

[k] 1 Peter 2:21

in daily life in a way that demonstrated faithfulness to His calling, and we are to do the same.

Bottom Line

Christianity as a vocation is a serious calling, and Jesus minced no words when describing the cost. "Whosoever he be of you that forsaketh not all that he hath, he cannot be my disciple."[1] Those words must have stunned His disciples, and men have struggled with them ever since. If you aren't sure what that looks like in your life, go back to the early church in the book of Acts. They understood that Christianity was a calling on their entire lives—everything was to be relinquished, nothing was exempt.

In the next few chapters we will take a closer look at some ways God intends our churches, homes, and businesses to wake up a spiritually apathetic culture that is trying to distance itself from God. Some of these areas may be difficult or even painful. It is so easy to understand that my unbelieving neighbor has an improper worldview, yet it is often difficult to grasp that my own incorrect worldview might be keeping him from examining his!

---

[1] Luke 14:33

CHAPTER 12

Church Communities That Care

Jesus said seekers will know they have found authentic Christianity when they discover local communities of believers demonstrating sacrificial love for each other.[a] Yet, looking at the religious landscape, one could assume Jesus had never commented on this topic. The church today is fragmented, more famous for schism and separation than for self-denying love and oneness, and the Anabaptists have been no exception. There are a number of reasons for this, and my goal is not to be too simplistic. But there are two questions churches today wrestle with that impact the unity in our brotherhoods. First, how should our families relate to the local church? And second, how much concern should

---

[a] John 13:35

we have about our unbelieving neighbor? In this chapter I would like to share some observations regarding these two areas.

The Family Church

In the book *Church Matters,* I addressed the issue of how we see the local assembly. There is a major difference between attending a church and committing to a church. On the continuum below, two church models are at opposite ends. Few churches, if any, are at either extreme, yet every fellowship is somewhere along this continuum.

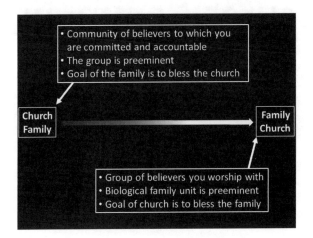

The family church is a gathering place for believers on Sunday mornings and possibly Wednesday nights. There are excellent sermons, enjoyable social functions, and various activities that families like to participate in. The primary goal of a family church is to bless and serve the biological family. There is a strong emphasis on family life, and on Sunday, families typically sit together during the service.[b] However, if another church seems to fit the family's needs better, it is not too difficult for the family to move its membership to that church. The family church provides a place where

---

[b] This is not intended to criticize fellowships who choose to sit as families. Rather, this can help in identifying where a congregation is on the continuum.

the biological family can worship and interact with other families who share a desire to serve the Lord. Loyalty to the church group is less of an emphasis than loyalty to the needs of the biological family. Consequently, it is not uncommon to discover that many within a family church have moved from another fellowship within the last five to seven years.

The Church Family

At the other end of the spectrum is the church family, or the church that becomes your family. In this model, the goal of the biological family is to bless and serve the church. The church is more than just a gathering place for saints, it is a community of believers who share their lives together. It is a place designed by God where people can know and be known, and love and be loved—a place where acceptance is extended because of Jesus, not due to who you are or what biological family you come from. There is also strong loyalty to the group, and long-term commitment is normal and expected. Wherever you find a church family, you will also find robust accountability and parameters that define membership—and those within are very aware where the lines of membership are.

> The church is more than just a gathering place for saints, it is a community of believers who share their lives together.

In his book *When the Church Was a Family,* Joseph Hellerman describes the strong family ties that bound biological families in first-century Mediterranean culture. "Family loyalty was an exclusive commitment. A person simply could not maintain descent-group[c] type loyalty to more than one family. The decision to join God's family invariably meant compromising to some degree the ties of loyalty that connected Jesus'

---

[c] Descent-group here is speaking of your ancestral lineage. It is the family you were born into.

followers to their natural families."[14] Grasping this powerful allegiance to line and lineage (almost impossible from our Western mindset) might help us understand why so much ink is used in the New Testament to address this topic. In Jesus' day, the family was preeminent!

For those of us growing up in an individualistic culture, this is difficult to grasp. When Jesus spoke of the ultimate test of allegiance for His followers, it was not personal freedom He put on the line. It was family loyalty. This was the ultimate test in His day.[d] "He that loveth father or mother more than me is not worthy of me," Jesus said, "and he that loveth son or daughter more than me is not worthy of me."[e] Absolute allegiance to your biological family was normal, expected, and was a huge part of who you were. But the beautiful reality about the early church was the fact that the church became their new family. When we read those first few chapters in Acts, it describes a group of people who interacted, communicated, and shared—like family!

This was the trademark of the Anabaptists coming out of the Reformation as well. When you came into the brotherhood, you accepted responsibility for not just your own actions, but also your brother's. The eighteenth chapter of Matthew regarding going to your brother when an offense arose was a command to follow. After all, you were now part of the family. Seeing the church as family has been a hallmark of the Christian church, but we are at risk of losing it. One of our goals should be to move our churches down the line on this continuum toward closer community. Our churches were intended to be families.

Evangelism

While the local church is intended to spend time together, work together, and share together just like a biological family, another

---

[d] Luke 14:26

[e] Matthew 10:37

feature is equally important. We are also to be actively reaching out to others and adopting them into Jesus' kingdom. Today's seekers will quite likely be an unmarried single parent, a divorcee struggling to navigate life while working and only seeing her children on alternate weekends, or simply someone coming from a dysfunctional home. If you are part of a family church, these people will have even more difficulty integrating into your congregation. They may never feel that they measure up.

The initial early church was a homogenous group of Jews. They had the same background, the same worldview, and a shared history. This enabled them to skip several steps in forming a church, as there were many issues they didn't even have to discuss or come to agreement on. Simply keeping their faith to themselves would have been the easiest path for the early church. But they didn't. As soon as it was revealed that the Gospel was for everyone, we see men and women intentionally crossing social, ethnic, and cultural lines to share what they had been given. They were busy sharing their faith, preaching to anyone who would listen, and even selecting and sending out men to evangelize. Sharing their newfound faith seems to have been the logical next step after becoming a follower of Jesus. Men and women heard the Gospel, believed the message, repented of their sins, were baptized, received the Holy Spirit, and immediately began sharing their faith with others. Outreach was simply the predictable consequence of initially receiving the Gospel. It still is today.

Go to any place on the globe where the Gospel has just been introduced, and you will find this replicated. I have never seen or heard of an exception. When people initially come to faith, they are overwhelmed by God's goodness, and it is difficult to keep them quiet. Even though speaking up has great risks, first generation Christians cheerfully hazard the peril of persecution to share the Gospel. The same Spirit that called them to repent now calls them to reach out. This is a very predictable pattern.

Yet there is also another corresponding historical corollary. Over time, churches lose that initial desire to share, and we become distracted and self-focused. Our gaze seems to turn from the many who don't know about Christ to the challenge of keeping the church organization itself operating smoothly. Today, there is a difference among our American Anabaptist churches regarding the importance of caring about our neighbors. Some churches are intentionally looking for opportunities to reach out, while others seem to have no interest at all. I have talked to individuals who see neighbors joining their local church as a threat or a potential problem, and some even try to discourage it.

With this in mind, let's add another aspect to the continuum we looked at earlier. At the top we have churches who are intentionally reaching out in their community, and at the bottom those who are not.

Examining Your Personal Perspective of Church

As you consider this chart, first take some time to place yourself personally on the horizontal continuum. Begin by examining your church commitment. How devoted are you to your local brotherhood? Are you

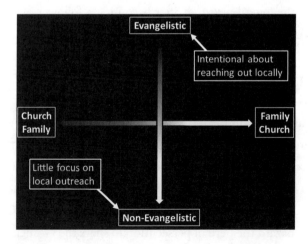

willing to submit to the counsel of others? Are you in this for the long haul, or do you see church membership as a fairly loose arrangement?

In our individualistic culture it is easy to slowly move away from anything that threatens my personal liberty. Finally we arrive at a point where church is a nice place to worship, interact, and be refreshed, but its primary purpose is to bless me and my family. Where are you on the church family versus family church continuum?

Now look at the vertical line. Where are you in your commitment to reach out to your neighbor? It is possible to be very involved in all kinds of evangelistic activities and serve on multiple outreach committees, yet ignore the people who live right next door.

Examining My Local Church

Also take some time to identify your local fellowship on these continuums. Does your local church operate like a family church where everyone gathers to enjoy a good message or a good meal and then returns home, or is it more like a biological family where there is serious commitment and accountability? A church family takes intentional steps to draw closer as a community.

Then consider where your church is in regard to outreach. A church that is engaged in reaching out to their neighbors will be praying for them, having frequent discussions about their needs, and be looking for ways to serve them. Adjustments will be made to the congregation's social calendar to enable interaction with them.

There is a general assumption in America that Christians do not care about anything other than their own people. Where your church is placed on these two continuums will impact your ability to provide disquieting exposure.

CHAPTER 13

A Closer Look

It may seem strange when discussing evangelism to focus on different ways of "doing church." But I suggest that few things will turn the average American's head as much as a church that demonstrates unconditional love among themselves while also being obviously interested in the seeker.

In this chapter I want to take a closer look at the continuums we created. We will take the chart and create four church models and try to learn from them. While illustrations and diagrams are usually incomplete, they can assist us in picturing and better grasping a basic truth. They can often take a complex situation and make it easier to understand and discuss. So with that disclaimer, let's create four basic church models from the chart in the last chapter and see what we can learn.[a]

Model 4

This church could be called the anemic church. Little commitment is

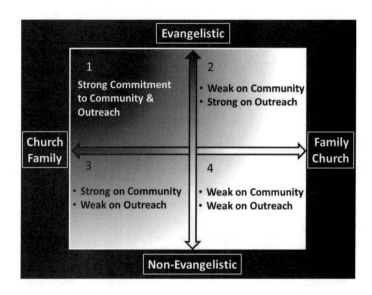

required to attend, and there is little interest in reaching out to others. While it may have excellent, well-delivered messages each Sunday, a serious seeker who is searching for a church similar to what he sees in the book of Acts will find something lacking. Weak on outreach and weak on community, this church makes its members feel good and asks little of them. There will be very little to attract a serious seeker.

Model 3

This church is strong on community but has no real interest in reaching out to others. If you belong to this church, your parents and grandparents were likely members here as well. Members in this church have

---

[a] In the book *Surviving the Tech Tsunami,* I looked at different church models and how they affect a church's ability to address technology. Those models were created by contrasting a church's emphasis on church community and Biblical teaching. This model contrasts the emphasis on church community and local evangelism.

a strong commitment to each other. Like the early church, the individual commits his life to the group, but the group also commits itself to the individual. Belonging to a church family provides a sense of security, and when a crisis comes, the individual faces it with the knowledge that he will be cared for. If a father is killed in an accident, for example, the group will encircle and care for the bereaved wife and children. If a barn burns down, the church family will gather and rebuild. In one sense that barn belonged to the farmer. But in another very real sense, that barn was also part of the church community.

Commitment to this church is usually lifelong, and leaving could carry significant social ramifications. It is not a church you casually join—or leave. In short, loyalty to this church is stronger than to the biological family.

However, this church has little interest in evangelizing their neighbors. When neighbors do come to the faith, it will likely be a relief to see them join another fellowship. A serious seeker may be drawn to the community aspect of this church, even recognizing strong similarity to the church he is reading about in the book of Acts. Yet most will quickly recognize that there are so many cultural barriers that committing will seem out of reach. Sometimes those who do join this model are more attracted to the community and culture than motivated by a spiritual desire to walk closer to Jesus. Integrating a serious seeker into a Model 3 is usually very difficult and can be frustrating, both to the seeker and the church community.

Model 2

This church is strong on outreach but weak on community. They probably have a kid's club, a prison ministry, and a mission board to organize projects and keep evangelism on the front burner. Most likely they provide tracts to their members and encourage them to share with their neighbors. Missionaries are invited to share their experiences on Wednesday nights, and flyers tacked to the bulletin board in the foyer provide mission updates. Collections are regularly taken to financially support various evangelistic endeavors around the globe and at the local soup kitchen. This church is obviously very interested in reaching out. But the members of this church seem to lack commitment to long-term church community. They enjoy the sermons, like the Bible studies, and appreciate belonging to a church that is actively seeking and reaching out to the lost, but one senses that their commitment doesn't run very deep. If they found another church nearby with better sermons or a more vibrant youth program, they would consider making the swap. They are strong on outreach, but weak on commitment to the group. Yet because they are interested in reaching out to others, seekers are more likely to be attracted to this church than to a Model 3.

Model 1

I would suggest this model is the rarest of all: a church where members have both a strong commitment to each other and a passion to reach out to the lost. They want to become closer as a community and frequently speak of Jesus' final request for the church: "That they all may be one; as thou, Father, art in me, and I in thee, that they also may be one in us: that the world may believe that thou hast sent me."[b] They firmly believe that oneness as a church will be a testimony to the world, and that this unity should imitate Jesus' closeness to His Father. "I in them, and thou in me, that they may be made perfect in one; and that the world may know that thou hast sent me, and hast loved them, as thou hast loved me."[c] They do not spend their time sitting around defining exactly how much submission to the local church is actually required. They just want to become more and more united as a church, and they see this self-sacrificing unity speaking loudly to a self-centered culture. Their personal lives are open to their brothers and sisters, and their homes are open to

---

[b] John 17:21
[c] John 17:23

their neighbors. This is the model that I believe Jesus desires.

"Great!" I hear you saying. "Where does this church exist and how can I become a part of it?" But before you call the moving company and desert your congregation, remember—the early church wasn't made up of special people. We don't read that the apostles carefully handpicked specific groups of believers to achieve this goal. The early church accomplished amazing things, but they were just common people who were committed to each other and to their Lord. So take another look at the people you worship with each Sunday. The refreshing and exciting reality is this: God is able to construct a vibrant church from ordinary people, and it is very possible you already have the ingredients right where you are!

Constant Migration

Before moving on, I want to point out another observation. There is a common and predictable migration across this chart. There seems to be a constant flow in our Anabaptist churches from a Model 3 to a Model 2.

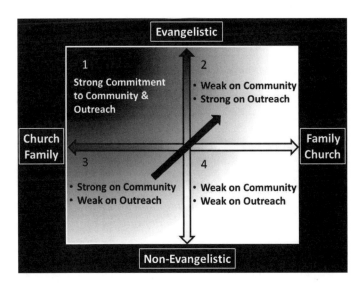

As individuals sense a lack of spirituality, little emphasis on the new birth, ungodly lifestyles or practices of some within the community, or perhaps the authoritarian methods used by the leadership, they become disillusioned. Most of us are familiar with situations where a steady diet of teachings on submission to authority, coupled with leaders who seemed to have little interest in the spiritual growth of their people, resulted in disillusionment. Consequently, individuals begin searching for a church with more spiritual emphasis, and they almost always move to a church with less focus on submission, fewer restrictions, and less emphasis on communal life.

My goal here is not to chastise this migration—nor to promote it. Sometimes it is essential to the spiritual vitality of the individual and his family. But it is important to understand what is being lost. I have talked to many people who have made this transition. After several years, they begin to realize that while the move may have been necessary, something of vital importance was lost in the process.

A Vision Worth Pursuing

God wants the church be more than just a place to gather for worship. It is to be a living and vibrant expression of God Himself to a dying world. It is to be a group of people both committed to each other and deeply dependent on the Spirit of God. If you are serious about reaching out to

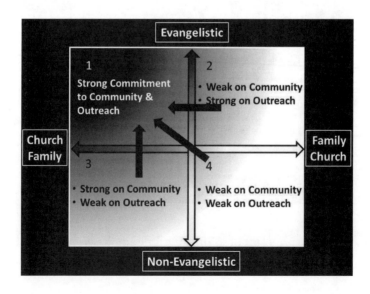

Reaching America

America, it is essential to grasp this basic truth. God still wants to reach out through a collective expression of self-sacrificing love.

I don't know of any church out there that would say they have arrived and are consistently loving each other and reaching the lost as Jesus intended. But don't let that keep you from visualizing what Jesus has in mind and from pressing toward that goal! If you are in a Model 2 church, reexamine your commitment to your local church community. Are you willing to submit to authority, lay down your life for your brother or sister, and move toward collectively living out a public demonstration of Jesus Christ through community?

If you find yourself in a Model 3 church, you have been blessed with a strong and vibrant church community. But remember, God didn't give you this tremendous gift to be hoarded. Jesus died so others can also experience what you have been given. God does not give gifts just for us to stockpile them. His eye is on the struggler down the road, and yours should be as well.

Mary is an older lady who has experienced many difficulties. She had been through several difficult relationships, was divorced, and out of desperation she began to seek the Lord. Mary knew nothing about Anabaptist churches, but she found a small fellowship close to her and began attending. "It was so beautiful," Mary told me. "These people loved each other, and they were everything I wasn't. They willingly sacrificed for each other, and I knew there was no way I could ever fit in. And even if they did accept me, I was sure I would ruin the loveliness of what they had!" Mary was simply experiencing the beauty of a church family. Yet even as they slowly drew her in, she remained convinced it would never work. Her past was simply too black and ugly, and she saw herself as someone these people would not want.

Time went on, they kept loving her, and Mary continued attending while feeling like an outsider attending a family reunion. But eventually she became convinced that they actually wanted her, and she became part of this church family. Years have passed now, and Mary has remained a faithful and happy member of this congregation. As she joyfully shared her story, Mary concluded with this comment: "They just wouldn't let me go!"

Sadly, it is rare for Americans to observe churches like this. Few have seen Christians willingly sacrificing their own wills and agendas for the good of their church community.

In summary, many churches have local outreach programs, and many operate as a family. But rarely do you find churches with both. But that is our calling, and it is a vision worth pursuing.

CHAPTER 14

Caring Like Jesus

J ust before going to the cross, Jesus engaged in an activity that caused His disciples to marvel. He knelt down and washed their feet. As Bible readers, we are all familiar with this account, but there is one significant detail we can easily miss: One of the men whose feet Jesus washed would soon turn against Him. And Jesus was fully aware of this. This simple truth tells us much about who Jesus is. There is something here for us to learn as we consider reaching out to others.

Have you ever become involved in a seeker's life, then suddenly discovered something about this person that made the possibility of him becoming part of your fellowship extremely unlikely? Maybe you have developed a relationship with a couple in your community. They have a nice family. They are eagerly asking for spiritual help, knowing they are lost and need the Lord, and they would like to start meeting to study the Bible.

Immediately you see the Lord's hand. Your excitement flares, they become the target of many prayers, and you are enthusiastic about the possibilities. Then you discover that this is not their first marriage, and your heart sinks. You know the chances of them being willing to live separately are close to zero. There is also the issue of their three children. What would happen to them? Our world is full of messy situations like this. But for our purposes, the question is this: How do you respond when you sense you may get nothing in return?

That was the situation Jesus faced that last night. Judas would soon be on his way to the priests to betray his Lord, yet Jesus washed his feet just as lovingly as He did Bartholomew's or Andrew's. He served Judas even though He knew He would receive nothing in return. Loving people who may never join our fellowship is an excellent way to give them a different picture of Christianity.

Examining Our Motives

One of the common accusations levied at Christians by skeptics today is that we are only motivated by a desire to increase church membership—that we will do whatever it takes to persuade people to join our group. They feel that churches, like secular organizations, are just money machines looking for increased numbers and a larger donor base. While increased financial revenue may not be driving our desire to reach out, it is essential that we examine our motives. Am I reaching out because of a genuine concern and compassion for the seeker? Or am I secretly hoping to receive something in return?

Joyce was a young woman who had been visiting different churches in our community. She didn't know much about Christianity and attended with a genuine desire to learn. But as she spent time interacting with different churches, she started to notice a pattern. People were initially very friendly and willing to answer questions. But after a while, when they sensed Joyce wasn't ready to join their fellowship, they began to distance themselves from her. Joyce was confused. It seemed the people were friendly only as long as there was hope she would join their group. They had time for her only as long as they were going to gain something in return.

If you really want to challenge a cynic's presuppositions, try loving unconditionally. That is disquieting exposure! Love him because he is created in the image of God—because God loves him and he has an eternal soul. We are surrounded by broken relationships, broken marriages, and broken lives. A follower of Jesus is drawn to brokenness. Not because of what we might receive in return, but because we long to see restoration. We reach out because we have a genuine interest in individuals and their lives, not to add more trophies to our congregational showcase. Success is seeing relationships restored and the lost found, even if they never set foot in our church. Our passion is to seek and save those who are lost. Following the example of Jesus, we invest time, show love, and even wash their feet, expecting nothing in return. Few things provide disquieting exposure like genuine love. It is capable of shaking even the most hardened skeptic.

> Few things provide disquieting exposure like genuine love. It is capable of shaking even the most hardened skeptic.

The Open Door of Human Suffering

As you interact with unbelievers, the topic of pain and suffering is common. It is frequently brought up as proof that an all-powerful, loving God cannot exist. "He may be all-powerful," the cynic will state, "or he may be loving, but he cannot be both. If a God existed that was both all-loving and all-powerful," unbelievers like Indy Cided will say, "human suffering would not exist."

All of us wrestle with human suffering, and there is much we don't understand. Why does God allow so much pain to exist? Why doesn't He just stop it? I have struggled with this issue, and yet I have learned to trust Him. I have seen His care and love in so many circumstances. I have seen enough that I am willing to trust Him for the situations I don't understand yet. And I have seen power and beautiful things come out of human suffering!

In his book *The Problem of Pain,* C. S. Lewis notes, "Pain insists upon being attended to. God whispers to us in our pleasures, speaks in our conscience, but shouts in our pains: it is His megaphone to rouse a deaf world."[15] As you think back over the life of Jesus and His daily interactions with humanity, what stands out? Go back through the Gospels. In what instances do we learn the most about His power and character? Was it not when He interacted with human suffering—the times He healed the lame, gave sight to the blind, and even interrupted funerals? Human grief and pain were the stage for so much of what Jesus did, and it provided the opportunity to demonstrate who He was. Can you imagine how lepers felt when Jesus touched them? How long had it been since any "clean" person had touched them? But Jesus didn't shrink from suffering. He purposefully entered into it with them.

Standing before the grave of Lazarus and surrounded by grief and sorrow, Jesus knew what would happen. He knew Lazarus would come forth in a few minutes, and the place would erupt in joyful exclamation. Yet He used this brief moment to enter into their pain. The shortest verse in the Bible succinctly reveals so much: "Jesus wept."[a] Wherever Jesus went, He seemed to search out human suffering and use it as a platform to demonstrate the character of God. The Christian church today should be doing the same. Human suffering is an open door of opportunity to reach out.

---

[a] John 11:35

Never Let a Crisis Go to Waste

In the aftermath of the 2008 American banking meltdown, the financial markets were in chaos and the situation for many looked bleak. Some even lost their homes. It was during this time that an Illinois Congressman made a surprising statement. "You never want a serious crisis to go to waste," he said.[16] In other words, this is a terrible crisis and a tragedy, but let's use it for political advantage. This quote was not original with him, as other politicians had previously expressed the thought. He was just putting words to a common political tactic—use disasters to your own personal advantage. Although politicians have used this technique many times for their own selfish means, I wonder if we can learn something.

Churches That Never Waste a Crisis

One of the characteristics I have observed in vibrant churches who effectively reach out is that they are both ready and watching for a crisis. They know that physical or emotional suffering can sometimes open closed doors. So when there is a major financial setback, a house fire, the death of a child, or some other unexpected emergency in the local community, these churches see it as an open door. They see it because they have been praying for an opportunity. Recently I observed a local church move into action when a neighbor discovered he had cancer and did not have long to live. The young people gathered to sing, the minister spent time speaking with him privately about his spiritual condition, and when he died the family turned to this church for help. This family had limited financial means, so the men from the congregation built a casket, and the church conducted the funeral. This family was literally overwhelmed. They had never experienced anything like this! They knew that the vast majority of the people in the church had never even met this young man before he died. *Why,* they wondered, *do these people even care about us?* What they were experiencing was the love of God through a church community. It also provided a rare opportunity for this family to not only hear the Gospel message but to also experience it. For a struggling family who thought they understood Christianity and felt no need for it, this was disquieting exposure!

I know of people who scan the newspaper each day just looking for individuals who may need help. They have seen God move through catastrophes and want to be available. However, churches that properly utilize a crisis don't just wait for one. They will be praying for and building relationships with their neighbors far in advance. They will be spending time with them, getting to know them, and showing them that God cares. They will be constructing bridges into their neighbors' lives so when the Lord allows the water of difficulty to rise, they will know where to go.

Situations like the 2020 coronavirus pandemic have provided excellent opportunities to be a neighbor. Many helped in food banks, made face masks, or just purchased groceries for elderly neighbors who were more vulnerable and susceptible to the virus. An older man who observed masked church youth assisting in a foodbank told one of them, "When I see you here, it tells me a lot about what kind of Christians you are, and what type of Christianity you come from." I don't know if this man was a Christian or not, but he definitely understood that there are differences in Christian groups. Helping out during a crisis is what Jesus meant by being a neighbor. Like the Good Samaritan, we should be looking for opportunities to help regardless of a person's background, ethnicity, or economic status. This is an excellent way to provide disquieting exposure!

Do You Know Your Neighbor?

How much thought have you given to the people who live close to you geographically? Do you know their names, their struggles, and the areas they would like you to be praying for them? Are they comfortable sharing their burdens with you? If they had a major difficulty and needed someone to share the load, would they knock on your door? If we are going to reach out to our neighbors, we will need to get acquainted.

It is so easy to get excited about a work project somewhere else, maybe even in a foreign country. But what about the people who live next door? Do we know what difficulties they are facing? This thought has challenged me many times. My neighbors all seem quite self-sufficient from a distance, and it is easy to assume they have little need of companionship. But when we spend a little time with them, a different picture may emerge. Behind all the material prosperity are many hurting hearts. So take a moment to consider your neighbors. Are you actively praying for them? I suspect you have made some assumptions about your neighbors. But do you really know them?

How Well Do Your Neighbors Know You?

Just as you have made some assumptions about your neighbors, they have also made some about you. The home you live in, the vehicle you drive, even the way you act when you drive past—all of this is speaking to them. They probably have a fairly good picture of your views and values simply by what they see. So what would they say is the most important thing in your life? Would they say you have time for them and have a concern for them? Maybe the real question is this: As they observe you and how you live, are your values and your love for them shaking up their assumptions about Christianity?

These can be sobering questions. We are often busy and our social schedules can become extremely full. We rush from meeting to meeting, from event to event, trying to decide which social functions are essential and which are not. Maybe it is time for us to stop and analyze what is driving our frantic schedules. Is my busyness really due to a love for the kingdom of God and a desire that my neighbor would experience God's love? Or am I being driven more by the social expectations of others and a fear of what people might think if I don't attend that particular function? We like to talk about putting everything on the altar—our families, our occupations, our finances. But if we don't have time to reach out to our neighbors and show them we care, maybe we need to rethink our social lives. I believe providing disquieting exposure in our neighborhood will require us to put our calendars on the altar as well.

CHAPTER 15

Placing Our Homes on the Altar

I grew up in a home where reading the Bible was a normal activity. My father did not use some preformatted study guide designed to make devotional life easier. We just read from the Word of God, discussed what we read, and talked about how the message should be applied in daily life. Since this was a regular occurrence, I grew up quite confident that I knew what the Bible said about most spiritual topics and religious doctrines. I was also exposed to frequent theological discussions. Even our extended family gatherings were times of religious dialogue, and it would have been a rare gathering that we didn't pull out our Bibles for reference. Oblivious to my spiritual swagger, I was sure I had a good grasp of what the Christian life should look like. I was confident we were doing things correctly—far too confident. Looking back, *arrogant* would not be too strong a word.

God can be very specific when He wants to be. Whether it was which toe the priest was to put blood on when cleansing a man[a] or describing the physical deformities that disqualified someone from serving as a priest,[b] God was not afraid to be precise in the Old Testament. Explicit instructions for their feasts and ceremonies told the Jewish people that God wants things done correctly. But when we turn to the New Testament there is a marked difference, a surprising lack of specifics. You can scan from Matthew to Revelation, but you will not find detailed instructions telling how to perform a marriage or ordain a church leader. Under the New Covenant, God seems to have given latitude, allowing individual churches the right to apply Scriptural principles using Holy Ghost discernment. That said, there are two important takeaways.

New Testament Application

First, we should exercise charity with other fellowships that are honestly trying to apply Biblical principles. Second, when the New Testament is specific, we should sit up and take notice. As a young man I failed to see this major difference between the Old and New Testaments. I saw God as a particular God who wants things done right, and I was excited about being part of a group that was doing it. I had little charity for those who saw things differently. But unknowingly, I wasn't paying much attention to some important commands of Jesus. I am constantly amazed at how many (and I keep discovering more) Scriptural teachings I find that I have previously given little thought to. Perhaps someone from a different church affiliation, or even a different religion, asks about a particular teaching or verse in Scripture that I have never placed much emphasis on. Suddenly I become aware that, once again, I have been oblivious to the obvious. For me, one of these overlooked areas was finding out

---

[a] Leviticus 14:28

[b] Leviticus 21:17-21

the way God intends for us to use our homes.

Kingdom-Focused Hospitality

Jesus did not give detailed instructions on the exact procedure we should use when observing communion, baptizing, or choosing a style of dress (issues that denominations have debated and divided over for years). But He did give explicit instructions on who we should be inviting into our homes, although it is rarely mentioned in church discussions. Pay close attention to these words of Jesus: "Then said he also to him that bade him, When thou makest a dinner or a supper, call not thy friends, nor thy brethren, neither thy kinsmen, nor thy rich neighbors; lest they also bid thee again, and a recompense be made thee. But when thou makest a feast, call the poor, the maimed, the lame, the blind: and thou shalt be blessed; for they cannot recompense thee: for thou shalt be recompensed at the resurrection of the just."[c]

When defending a particular doctrinal truth or practice that we promote, I have often heard someone say, "This Scripture is so clear that even a child could understand it." What we are subtly implying is, "If others were as serious about following Jesus as we are, they would just do what it says." We like this logic when referring to doctrines like nonresistance or the woman's head veiling. But let's get back to the verses we just quoted. What would a child say this teaching of Jesus means? What is He saying?

Jesus was very thorough in His wording here. There is really no wiggle room in His instructions about who we should invite into our homes. He was describing kingdom-focused hospitality. Jesus told us who *not* to invite (your friends who can reciprocate). He told us who we *should* invite (the poor or people different from you). And He told us *why* we should do this (to bless others, not ourselves). Reciprocation comes later.

---

[c] Luke 14:12-14

These are very clear instructions on how to generate a guest list. For some of us, obeying Jesus' words might simply mean inviting members from our own church who have few friends or are difficult to get along with. It might mean providing hospitality to an elderly couple who cannot return the favor. But one message is clear: We are to use our homes to bless those who cannot repay us.

God, speaking through Isaiah, had similar words when describing the type of sacrifice acceptable to Him. "Is it not to deal thy bread to the hungry, and that thou *bring the poor that are cast out to thy house?* when thou seest the naked, that thou cover him; and that thou hide not thyself from thine own flesh?"[d] (Emphasis mine.)

Sacrificial Hospitality

I don't suppose Isaiah's Jewish audience liked this message any better than Jesus' listeners liked His. In fact, both audiences might have been a little scandalized by the suggestion. And let's be honest; maybe we find uncomfortable thoughts about this rolling around in our minds as well. *Bring society's losers into my house? Really? I don't mind writing an occasional check to a homeless shelter, but bringing dirty, smelly misfits inside my nice, clean home? No way!*

But before we dismiss these words of Jesus outright, shouldn't we at least consider what He might have had in mind? I don't believe Jesus intended for us to harbor individuals who are dangerous or who might be a threat to our children. I will address that issue later. Neither was Jesus saying we should carelessly associate with those with poor morals. James provided clear warning on this topic. "Know ye not that the friendship of the world is enmity with God? whosoever therefore will be a friend of the world is the enemy of God."e But I do believe God wants our homes to be open and to be used purposefully. Jesus

---

[d] Isaiah 58:7

[e] James 4:4

specifically said we are to invite the poor, the maimed, the lame, and the blind. These are people with limitations and difficulties. They will require something of us, and working with them will be a sacrifice that produces little, if any, immediate recompense.

All of us like to be invited. There is something special about being selected to attend an event. It makes us feel we have worth, that someone thinks we are of value. Many of us know how to get more invitations—just have lots of company in our home. People come, enjoy themselves, and then they return home knowing that cultural courtesy demands that they reciprocate. We enjoy this closed cycle of hospitality, but the words of Jesus are a clear command to open that cycle. Our homes, like everything else we possess, are to be put on the altar. No longer are our homes simply for our own pleasure and enjoyment. They are to be committed to and used for God's glory and purposes. I suggest they are one of the most powerful platforms for outreach God has given us.

> Our homes, like everything else we possess, are to be put on the altar.

On Enemy Soil

Kenneth Smith was pastor of a small church in Syracuse, New York. For years his church had been praying for and reaching out to the students and staff of nearby Syracuse University. In an effort to develop a relationship and better inform students about Christianity, Ken had written a letter to an English professor. Surprisingly, she responded, and Ken invited this professor, Rosaria Butterfield, to his home. This initial contact was the beginning of an ongoing dialogue and relationship that neither of them could have predicted.

Rosaria came to Ken's home that night as an avowed atheist. Not only that, she was a feminist, a lesbian, and a vocal activist within the gay community. She pulled into the driveway with many presuppositions about Christianity. She saw evangelicals as obnoxious, conceited, shallow-minded, and unloving to anyone who opposed them. Her opinion about Christians was based on her own observations. She had seen these people carrying hate-filled signs at gay pride parades.

In her own words, she writes:

> Christians seemed like a small-minded, uncharitable, immoral bunch. They ate meat, believed in corporal punishment, violated human and environmental rights at a fevered pitch, denied a woman's right to choose, and believed that the whole world should fall under totalitarian obedience to the Bible, an ancient book fraught with racism, sexism, and homophobia.[17]

Rosaria was confident she had a good grasp of Christianity, and so far nothing had caused her to question her perspective. Until, that is, she walked into Ken Smith's living room. She arrived with confidence. Her butch haircut and car plastered with gay and pro-choice bumper stickers left little doubt about her philosophy in life. That one evening, however, shattered some basic assumptions.

Ken and his wife Floy did not fit her stereotype of Bible-thumping evangelicals. They seemed sincerely friendly and unashamedly prayed a simple prayer before the meal. They did not debate, yet they asked good questions and were excellent listeners. Rosaria waited all evening for the "evangelistic pitch," but it never came. They didn't even invite her to church. Despite their obvious differences, they treated her with dignity and respect. In the end, she was not sure what to do about them. She had no interest in the Jesus she thought she knew, but she found the Jesus she saw lived out in simple hospitality strangely attractive. Rosaria had experienced disquieting exposure!

She left that evening with some unsettling questions. Ken and Floy's kindness and concern for her as a person had disarmed her, and Rosaria continued coming to their home for meals and discussions. Two years of interaction with Ken and Floy would pass before Rosaria attended church. But these encounters caused her to begin asking some basic questions. *Do I really understand Christianity as well as I thought I did? Is it possible that God actually exists? And if so, what does He expect from me?*

An open home and basic hospitality opened her mind to the Gospel, and she eventually came to find Jesus for herself. She abandoned her ungodly lifestyle and even wrote a book describing her path to faith, *The Secret Thoughts of an Unlikely Convert.*[18] Today Rosaria is married with a family of her own, and as you can imagine, she has some opinions on how to reach out. In her own words, she was an unlikely convert. Although I would not necessarily agree with all of her theology, she seems like someone we should listen to when considering effective evangelistic approaches.

In 2018, Rosaria wrote a second book. This time she wrote from the perspective of a busy housewife, and the message of her book is that our homes are being underutilized. Reading this book, *The Gospel Comes with a House Key,*[19] can be a little overwhelming. It seems someone is always coming or going, stopping in unexpectedly for a meal, or coming over to drink coffee and share a concern. The pace is exhausting, and I have heard housewives say just reading it makes them tired. While not everyone is cut out for the hectic schedule outlined in this book, we should not ignore the overriding message: Jesus wants us to use our homes to extend hospitality to those living on the margins of society.

Taking Inventory

How has this basic command of Jesus influenced your life? How often do you host a stranger, someone unable to reciprocate, or just a neighbor who needs the Lord? During the past few years I have talked to many followers of Jesus who have an interest in evangelism, and I have been amazed how often I hear them say they rarely, if ever, have unbelievers in their home for a meal. Yet we are surrounded by broken people who desperately need Christ. Many of these have never experienced a home life where love and hospitality abound, so this is a great opportunity to demonstrate Jesus. Our homes are a great, untapped resource in reaching out to others. The testimony of people like Rosaria confirms this truth.

Jesus also told His followers to visit other homes. When sending out His disciples, He told them to take no provisions with them, but to enter into local homes and depend on them for necessities.[f] Here is another lesson to learn. We are called not only to provide hospitality but to receive it as well. There is something powerful about eating someone else's food in their home. It shows that you respect them as they are, that they have abilities God can use, and that you have basic needs in your life just as they do. It can be a tremendous way to build a relationship.[g] We Anabaptist people can appear very self-sufficient. But when we are willing to receive from others, it demonstrates that we are made out of the same stuff. We are just people too.

As I look at my own life and my interaction with my neighbors, I am ashamed at how much growth is needed. It is so easy to give to neighbors, but what about receiving? Take inventory of your life. How often do you eat in the home of someone in your neighborhood who comes from a different background? How might sitting around their dinner table affect your relationship? Some of these situations can be challenging, or even awkward. Children need to be taught to respect others even when people's cleanliness is not what they are used to. Here again, we don't want to invite neighbors into our homes just so they will invite us to theirs, but hospitality should go both ways. There should be times when we are blessed by those outside our church community. It is an excellent way to build essential relationships if local evangelism is going to occur.

---

[f] Matthew 10:11-15; Mark 6:7-11; Luke 9:1-6

[g] While occasional interactions are a blessing, care needs to be taken, especially with small children. Allowing them to be left alone or have unsupervised access to technology can be dangerous. It is much easier to maintain control of activities, influence, and atmosphere when entertaining in our own home.

Throughout Scripture, God has called His people to sacrifice the things that are of the most value to them. In the Old Testament they were to select a perfect animal and bring only the best to the altar. When Jesus came, He emphatically declared that a man could not even be His disciple without relinquishing His own family. Each time God calls for sacrifice, He fingers the item closest to our hearts and asks us to abandon it. When we consider the cost of opening our homes to those who cannot, for whatever reason, repay us, it may seem a high price indeed. For many of us, our homes are our most treasured possession, and choosing to place our home on the altar is not an easy decision.

There are families, however, within our conservative Anabaptist communities who have committed themselves to following this simple teaching of Jesus. They understand that their unbelieving neighbors are subconsciously searching for a blessing their family can provide, and in an effort to reach out they regularly open their homes to these people. I have interviewed some of these families and will share some of their struggles in another chapter.

I have also interviewed people who joined the Plain churches because someone opened their home to them in the past. They have been impacted by simple hospitality, and it has been inspiring to listen to their testimony. We will meet one of these families in the next chapter. I don't know how you use your home, and I acknowledge this concept may be difficult, but this is a very simple teaching of Jesus. Inviting the struggler into our home may sound as strange as nonresistance does to many of our Protestant friends. But allow yourself to consider the possibilities.

Our churches have a powerful testimony of assisting those who have experienced traumatic disasters. We show up when earthquakes hit, house fires destroy, or floods devastate entire communities. We are famous for helping after a tragedy or catastrophe, and this is an excellent way to demonstrate Jesus. But are we building relationships with the dysfunctional family who lives down the road? This command of

Jesus calls us to be a neighbor to everyone, but especially to those who have nothing of value and no way to repay. Imagine the impact if each of us would simply obey this command, right where we live!

CHAPTER 16

"They Drew Us In!"

It has been over thirty years now, but Edward can still remember sitting around that dinner table. He still has vivid memories of the blond-haired, blue-eyed children, the lively discussion, and getting down on the floor and playing with those youngsters after the meal. Edward spent many wonderful evenings in that home, but the thing he remembers most isn't the food, the discussions, or even the fun he had playing with the children. His most enduring memory is the way this family made him feel.

Edward was raised in a stable home surrounded by a supportive family. He enjoyed good friends, good health, and a good school. Since his father was the owner of a successful business, he grew up with advantages that many can only wish for. After graduating from college, Edward landed a good job and married his childhood sweetheart, Emma. Things could not have looked brighter for the two of them. Emma became a flight attendant for Delta Airlines, and with two incomes the future looked wonderful. In Edward's own words, he was living the American dream.

Edward and Emma purchased a small farm about half an hour west of where they had grown up and soon discovered they had some interesting neighbors. It was the first time either of them had come in direct contact with conservative Anabaptist people, and they were both strangely intrigued. While the plain dress was unlike anything they had been accustomed to, there was something else about this family that they couldn't quite put their finger on. Edward was new to farm life and occasionally stopped in to ask a question or discuss a dilemma. Each time he would come away more fascinated. Who were these people and what did they have that was so unique?

Emma's job as a flight attendant often took her away from home for days at a time, so sometimes after work Edward would stop in to chat with the neighbors. The family had dairy cows, and after he helped them do the chores, they would invite him in for supper. He thoroughly enjoyed those evenings.

"If I try to explain how they made me feel," Edward told me recently, "I would say they just made me feel like I belonged. Even though our lives were so different, they made me feel at home. I never felt like an outsider; they never made me feel awkward."

Whenever Emma returned home from a flight, Edward would share his experiences, and both of them began interacting more with the family. Before long they were invited to family birthday parties and church picnics and discovered this wasn't the only family like this. When Edward needed some construction work done, he asked these new friends for a recommendation and soon found himself working beside these people in the workplace. Again, something was different.

Something Is Different!

"All my life I had been taught that there are certain virtues that are good, such as using clean language, being honest, and being kind to others. I grew up hearing about these things, but the people around me weren't actually doing them. These people did! They practiced these virtues in their daily life in the workplace!"

As Edward and Emma continued to interact with these people, they wanted to know more. What was behind this different way of life? To find out, they began attending church and reading the Bible to verify what they were hearing. Eventually they came to know Jesus Christ in a new way and committed themselves to following the Lord. Emma gave up her job as an airline attendant, and they began raising a family within a conservative Anabaptist church community. In Jesus they had discovered the power behind this family that had drawn them in. Today, years later, Edward and Emma look back with gratitude. Here was a family who took the time to reach out and make them feel welcome. Asked to share what this has taught him over the years, Edward shared some insightful thoughts.

"People ask, 'Wasn't it difficult to make such a drastic change?' I tell them to go home and read in the *Martyrs Mirror* about the persecution the early Anabaptists went through. What those people did was hard. But putting on a plain suit—or to stop wearing shorts? That's really kind of trivial! Yes, there were changes. We got rid of our television, we made changes in how I did business, and I changed some of the language I used. Some of this can be a slow process, and I am still growing."

As you can imagine, Edward carries a burden for the lost and can identify with them. Today he operates a store that hires fellow Anabaptists and is visited by many tourists.

"When I see tourists come in, I watch how they gaze at the modestly dressed employee behind the counter, and a certain look comes across their faces. I know exactly what they are thinking," Edward said with a smile. He knows because he remembers having the same thoughts.

"I don't know how to explain the feeling. There is a certain wholesomeness and humility that is very compelling. There is also something attractive to seekers about seeing people connected to something larger than themselves. This is intriguing to a lot of people in our self-centered culture."

Where Is the Joy?

However, Edward isn't blind to flaws in the conservative Anabaptist community, and when asked, he is willing to share. Having experienced a wide variety of groups, he sees some areas in Anabaptist churches that need improvement, especially in outreach.

"I love the modesty and way of life of the conservative people. But sometimes there is also a sobriety and an aloofness that isn't attractive. I am not saying we should be giddy or silly—I am just talking about being approachable. Some groups can be very hard to approach. It is almost as though they don't know how to smile. 'Where is the joy?' people ask. 'Doesn't the Bible say Christians should be joyful?' "

Edward is also concerned about some condescending attitudes he's seen.

"Sometimes you get a sense from some of our people that they have arrived, and that they are in some way superior to others. We all know this is wrong. Yet sometimes this is the impression people get." Edward has strong feelings on this topic. Since he is committed to using his business to reach out, he spends time teaching on this topic when hiring new employees from the surrounding Anabaptist community.

Business as Mission

"I teach new employees to be friendly and to take time for questions whenever possible. I remind them that they have been given something of great value, and they should regard it as a gift. They don't realize what they have, and I try to help them see this. The fact that they were born into a family that sings together, memorizes Scripture, and belongs to a stable church community is a tremendous gift! God wants them to share what they have been given. I encourage my employees to be friendly to the man with tattoos and earrings, or to that lady who is dressed immodestly. These are people who haven't been given the same gifts we have."

A public business provides many chances to demonstrate Jesus, and Edward wishes more would use this opportunity.

"For the last thirty years I have worked and interacted with all kinds of Anabaptists. Some are very friendly and approachable, while others seem to hunker down and ignore those outside their group. They probably believe that the return of the Lord is near, and they don't want to lose any of their own people. I don't agree with this view, but as our culture becomes more ungodly, I understand it. We need to be careful we do not compromise our convictions or application of Scripture, because that is what we have to offer. If we lose that, we are done. I want my children to be excited and thankful about what they have!"

Edward paused a moment. "Yet we need to share what we have been given. I always stop and think—what about me? Where would I be and where would my family be if my neighbors hadn't reached out?"

> We need to share what we have been given.

If I Can Do It, Anyone Can!

It comes as no great surprise that Edward and Emma, in addition to using their business to reach out, have also been purposeful in how they use their home. Years before they opened their store, they found creative ways to interact with the public. They opened a bed and breakfast on their farm, and this brought in people from different parts of the United States and even from other countries. In the morning they would invite their guests to eat breakfast with them, then take them out to the barn and let them help feed a calf or the chickens. It wasn't uncommon for guests to ask questions, and this provided an excellent opportunity for their children to learn how to interact and respond. After visiting a while, they would sing. Edward and Emma's family enjoyed singing, and they saw this as one more way to share with people who were seeking.

"It may not be realistic to expect the masses to do what we have done, and our primary goal shouldn't be to just get people to join our church. If we can point others to Jesus and someday see them in heaven, I believe we will have been faithful. I am so excited about what we as conservative people have to offer the world! And the more volatile the world becomes, and as more people search for stability and simplicity, I think we could see an influx of people expressing interest in our groups."

I had begun the interview by explaining a little about the book I was currently writing and asked Edward what kind of encouragement he would give the Anabaptist people.

"We were met with grace and an open home, and we found ourselves drawn in. But the Holy Spirit was at work as well. We saw a wholesomeness that was hard to ignore. I think that is what drew the crowds to Jesus. There was something there that people longed for. Something radiated from Him that was hard to resist, and that is what happened to us as well. We had everything a person longs for. We both had good jobs, and we had a good family, yet we didn't have the most important thing. There are millions and millions of people like us out there. If we can do it, there are others who can too!"

CHAPTER 17

Intentional Hospitality

The Anabaptist people are known for hospitality. Having visitors in our homes, sharing meals, enjoying time together—these are common attributes among our church communities. But increasingly, young families are taking a closer look at the words of Jesus and attempting to go beyond inviting those who will reciprocate. Sometimes this means focusing on difficult situations right in their own congregations, but it does not have to be limited to that. These people also use their homes to reach out to people outside their church—perhaps unconverted neighbors or people who are going through difficult times.

This looks different in each home. Some have a more urban focus, while others live in rural settings. In this chapter I would like to peek into three homes that utilize different approaches. Yet they have one thing in common: They are demonstrating intentional hospitality. Hopefully we can be encouraged by their example.

Tom and Sally

Tom has always had an interest in other countries and cultures. Even though he had not traveled much himself, he wanted to broaden his children's horizons, so he decided to have them learn a second language. Looking for a tutor, Tom and Sally visited a nearby college to see if they could locate someone interested in a side job of tutoring. The college was a few miles away, and they found both older students and staff who were interested. This initial contact has changed their lives in ways they could not have predicted.

They began to develop friendships and eventually began inviting professors and students into their home. Today some of them are frequent visitors. They have entertained atheists and agnostics, as well as people of other religions, such as Buddhists, many of whom had experienced little or no other contact with Christians. Tom and Sally's goal is simply to love them and show them what a Christian family looks like. In Tom's words, "Our goal is to be their friend. We are just a normal family, and we are asking them to come join us. We want them to know that we care."

One student brought her professor along to visit, and throughout the evening the professor kept saying, "You have a wonderful family. I must bring my fiancé to see this! You must teach him how to raise children!" Tom told the professor this would be fine, and later he came along. He kept asking questions about the "secret" to raising a nice family. He asked about homeschooling and child training, and marveled that they had no television. Inviting people from the college has opened Tom and Sally's eyes to the great hunger in our society for answers. They are convinced that many people in our culture are searching for godly values.

At the conclusion of our visit, Sally summarized it like this: "There is so much potential in simply letting people observe our homes. When it is a godly home and Christ is there, there is so much for them to see."

Bob and Suzanne

Bob and Suzanne's approach is different. Bob grew up in the country, and his parents always carried a concern for the plight of low-income children in the nearby city. Consequently, they made frequent trips, developed relationships, and occasionally brought children back to the farm to enjoy a little country life. This early exposure influenced Bob, and after marrying Suzanne they continued this practice. After a few years of marriage, they decided to move into a low-income area of the city to increase their influence and ability to reach out. This move brought an abundance of challenges as well as opportunities, and they have many stories about these years.

Children would appear on their doorstep at all hours of the day or night. Some had not eaten a good meal for some time, and others were being neglected emotionally, their unconcerned parents off at the local nightclub. One child stayed in their home for several weeks before her apathetic parents came looking for her.

There was also abuse. One day a little girl came running into their home hollering that a boyfriend was hitting her mother. Bob, trying to think of an appropriate response, grabbed a socket wrench from the garage and quickly followed her back to her home. Running into the house behind the little girl, he held up the socket and interrupted the angry encounter. "James, would you have a socket a little larger than this one that I could borrow?" This was enough to divert the angry man and temporarily defuse the situation.

Bob and Suzanne tried various ways of developing relationships, and one of them was opening a neighborhood café. There was no charge, but neighbors could contribute if they wished. Suzanne and her daughters liked to cook, so they let everyone in the community know that Friday evening was café night. Neighbors would gather, the family would serve food, and then they would sing before opening up the evening for discussion. Bob was a minister, and the last twenty to thirty minutes concluded with an event he called "Stump the Pastor." Anyone could ask any difficult question, and Bob would attempt to answer. Sometimes there weren't many questions, but other times this resulted in a lively discussion. One man who came sometimes attempted to hijack the discussion as a platform to share his unbiblical perspectives. As a result, he was eventually asked not to return.

There were often thirty or forty neighbors who showed up for café night, and this took a toll on Bob and Suzanne's finances. Bob confessed that there were times they had to dip into their tithe money to keep going. They kept this project going for around ten years, until health issues forced them to stop. Bob looks back on this time and believes it was a blessing to both the neighbors and his family. Today about a third of the members of their city church are from a non-Anabaptist background. As I concluded the interview with Bob, he left me with a simple purpose statement for their home and their efforts in the city through the years. "Jesus said we should invite the people who can't repay us, and we were just trying to do what He said."

Frank and Elaine

Frank and Elaine live far away from the city. Surrounded by farmland, one could assume their opportunity for ministry or outreach would be limited. But if you were to peer into their home on an average weeknight, you might be surprised. As I talked with them, I was inspired by the creative ways they have allowed God to use their home.

Frank is a mechanic. Seeing opportunity in his occupation, he built a small shop on his property, stocked it with tools, and began doing mechanical work for the neighbors if they had a need. Neighbors with financial struggles started bringing their vehicles and asking for assistance. Many times this happened in the evening, and if it was around suppertime, Frank invited them in to join the family. This has led to many interactions and opportunities to build relationships. But of course, having an open home also comes with challenges.

One evening Frank was helping a man who had an extremely foul mouth. The man seemed incapable of completing a sentence without using inappropriate language. Frank had small children, so before bringing the man in for supper he warned his children. "This man isn't a believer, and you may hear some bad language." But to Frank's amazement, the man never swore or said anything unsuitable. Frank concluded that we often underestimate the power of a godly home and family on the worst of men.

Frank and Elaine have tried other ways of reaching out. Frank invited one young man from work to spend the evening. This young man started bringing his friends, and soon others wanted to come. Seeing young people who were craving wholesome interaction, they started inviting youth from the local town every Tuesday evening. Upon arriving, the youth were pointed to a large bowl with a sign proclaiming "More SOCIAL, Less MEDIA" and were instructed to put their phones into the bowl. At first this was a shocker. *Give up my phone?* But after relinquishing this prized possession, these young people discovered something. They *could* survive, and even have an enjoyable evening, without technology! They played table games, word games, and even enjoyed a mystery supper. At the end of the evening, Frank and Elaine had family devotions as they normally would. Not because youth were there, but because that was part of their normal routine.

As I listened to Frank and Elaine share ways they have built relationships with many local people, I could not help but be inspired by their low-key, grassroots approach. This is within reach of anyone! After they had shared some of the situations they had confronted, I asked how they would encourage others who wanted to begin doing this. Elaine paused before responding.

"I would tell them it isn't necessarily easy, but you have to decide what life is all about. Each family has to determine what their goals are. If your goal is to reach out to people, then you need to be willing to deal with the hard parts of it. It's not all fun."

Frank talked about some of the challenging situations they have experienced. "Prayer is so important! There have been times when it became clear in working with a relationship issue that it was a spiritual battle." After a pause he added, "But our people need to open their homes, and they can start small. Tell them to begin by doing it one evening a week."

Elaine chimed in with a final summary. "We are not Jesus, and we can't fix everyone's problems. But we can point them to Jesus. Our job is just to be there for people!"

Nothing in Return

These three families are from different areas, employing different approaches. But if you noticed, there are several things they have in common. First, they are taking the command of Jesus very seriously. They believe that when Jesus commanded us to invite people into our homes from outside our comfortable demographic strata, He actually meant what He said.

Second, each of them has been willing to invest in this vision. Our homes tend to be our private retreat, a place where we withdraw from the ugliness, the ills, and the problems of society. But these three families have chosen to bring "the poor, the maimed, the lame, the blind"[a] into the sanctity of their home, that quiet haven we love to protect. Though acknowledging there is risk, they have purposefully placed their homes on the altar.

---

[a] Luke 14:13

We might wonder if Jesus actually realized what He was asking. Didn't He understand that bringing sinful people into our homes might pose a threat to our children? But Jesus didn't say, "Invite the poor, the maimed, the lame, the blind; *as long as they are righteous people.*" No, it was an open-ended command, and the common denominator was that they give us nothing in return.

So what about the risk? What about the potential danger to our children? If you are a godly parent, you have already been wrestling with this issue, and we will consider it in the next chapter. After all, abuse has occurred in homes with well-meaning but inattentive parents. But don't let the potential risk blind you to Jesus' command. He understands and is able to provide protection for those who choose to obey, and He will guide those who have a sincere desire to bless others.[b]

---

[b] Throughout this section we are addressing Jesus' command to invite the underprivileged or those who are seeking for truth. This is not an encouragement to invite those who are attempting to proselytize. In 2 John 1:10 and 11, the Apostle John wrote, "If there come any unto you, and bring not this doctrine, receive him not into your house, neither bid him God speed: for he that biddeth him God speed is partaker of his evil deeds." He is warning us against encouraging or blessing those who are spreading false doctrines and attempting to convert us.

CHAPTER 18

Boundaries, Balance, and Blended Efforts

As parents, it is essential to maintain close control over the influences that come into our homes. So how can we do this while simultaneously opening our homes to people with very different worldviews? To get some ideas from parents who have done this, I asked them, "What are some challenges you have experienced, and what are some boundaries you would suggest?" I was blessed by their transparency, not only in sharing the good experiences, but also in admitting the challenges they faced and the mistakes they made. They all had failures to share.

In this chapter we are going to look first at boundaries some families have established, then consider the need for balance between the needs of others and the needs of our own children. Finally, we will look at the importance of being united in vision and working together, both within the family and in the church community.

Essential Boundaries

Every family I talked with stressed the importance of implementing clear lines of expectation for visitors. One father who invites many college students to his home is especially mindful of technology. "When I see someone's phone come out, my antenna goes up. We do not allow visitors to play videos or surf the internet in front of the children. I just tell them we don't do that in our home, and the students have always been very respectful."

Another couple expressed concern about allowing their children to be alone with guests. "Many visitors come to our home. But there are some we wouldn't ever leave our children alone with, not even in the living room. If we have families visiting our home and their children come along, we do not ever allow closed doors. Our children know this is not an option."

Another mother made this comment: "There are people who are welcome in our home, but we wouldn't allow our children to go anywhere alone with them."

One family who goes to a university frequently to interact with students said, "We don't allow our children to go anywhere alone. When on campus, we don't even allow a child to go to the restroom alone. If a sister or brother isn't available to go along, one of us parents will."

Each family I interviewed spoke of the need to constantly be aware of what is happening. Parents must be alert. Some families have a debriefing meeting after certain visitors leave. As one parent said, "It's an excellent time to go back over the conversations and make sure the children are aware of ungodly worldviews that were expressed. These discussions can be invaluable teaching moments. We want our children to develop their own alertness system."

One father who often works with immoral individuals said there are some people he does not invite into their home. "There are other places I can meet those individuals if I sense it would be too confusing for our children."

Another question I asked was, "Has anything ever happened or been said that you believe was harmful to your child?" Most have had uncomfortable circumstances but said they were able to walk back through the situation later with their children.

One said that after situations like that they get out their Bibles and address what happened from a Biblical perspective. "We talk about it and pray about it. These situations don't really concern me a lot. My children are going to be exposed to all this eventually anyway, and I would rather walk through each situation with them in our own home."

Insulated versus Isolated

As I listened to families who are using their home to reach out, it struck me that there is a difference between insulating our families from the filth in our society and isolating them from the world. Jesus addressed this just before going to the cross. "I pray not that thou shouldest take them out of the world, but that thou shouldest keep them from the evil."[a] In this prayer, Jesus repeatedly expressed His desire that the world would see the beauty of His people. This cannot occur when we remain isolated. You cannot reach out to your neighbors or show them the beauty of the kingdom if you are huddled inside your house and refuse to spend time with them.

Although God is not calling us to isolation, He does want us to be careful and use spiritual discernment. If you have children in your home, you must give thought to their well-being, the influence on their lives, and their spiritual safety.[b]

But don't let these concerns stop you from reaching out! I don't know of anything more powerful or effective in our culture than a well-ordered home. Obedient, happy, and fulfilled children will soften the most hardened heart,

---

[a] John 17:15

[b] Age of children needs to be taken into account. We have found that visitors tend to be very conscious of dressing inappropriately when visiting. However, many have been raised with very different standards and if provocative dress becomes an issue, parents will need to use discretion.

> I don't know of anything more powerful or effective in our culture than a well-ordered home.

and there are many hard hearts out there that need softening.

All the parents I spoke to agreed that the positive aspects of having their children exposed to those raised differently far outweighs the negative.

Balance

One of the primary concerns of individuals who are not accustomed to having unbelievers in their home is the impact on children, and that is definitely a valid concern. When I talk to those who regularly have neighbors around their dinner table, the word I hear most frequently is *balance*. In their opinion, the biggest issue is not bad influence on children as much as the possibility of neglecting their own families. The needs in many of our neighbors' lives are so great that parents can easily sacrifice their own children in an effort to help others. As one father said, "Once hurting people discover your home is open, they will come. And we can't have people in our home all the time. We must have time for our children."

Most of us struggle with balance, and it is easy to take on too much. I spoke with several parents who have addressed this dilemma by setting certain evenings aside as "family only" nights. In homes where people are accustomed to just dropping in, this might mean taking the family for a drive and stopping somewhere for supper. One family with teenage children does this occasionally, providing a time when they can talk and ask any questions.

This father, who raised his family in the middle of a metropolis, said it like this: "On the one hand, I wanted to win the city. But on the other, we have an Anabaptist culture I wanted to preserve and give to our grandchildren. It can be a delicate balance knowing where all the boundaries should be, and it is essential that parents, especially when living in the city, maintain very open lines of communication with their children." This father also purposefully took his sons on an extended hiking trip in the summer, with a goal of staying close to them.

Continuous communication seems to be the key for those who have done this successfully. One father who has dealt with individuals with major moral issues said, "We have tried to be very open with our children, explaining what is wrong with what these people are doing. I don't want my children to ever assume I condone these people's actions simply because they are welcome in our home."

Another father, while describing some of the scenarios they have dealt with, said, "There have been times we have needed to discuss some of these situations with our children. We want them to embrace the vision and feel like they are part of the team. We want them to grow up understanding that reaching out to others is simply part of the Christian life."

Blended Efforts

Intentional hospitality requires more than an enthusiastic father or an energetic, outgoing mother. Everyone needs to be involved. One father spoke of the importance and blessing of having your children engaged in the battle. "If your children understand that you are in a battle that's worth fighting, they will want to join you in the battle." One night he heard his six-year-old son weeping, so he went to his bedroom, assuming he had an upset stomach. "Daddy, so many of our neighbors are lost and going to hell! What are we doing about it?" This little boy was not very old, yet he had grasped his family's vision and wanted to be involved.

Intentional hospitality, over the long haul, can be very wearing on a wife. As mothers are well aware, there is always plenty to do. A healthy, happy home with children means that sticky goo mysteriously appears in the strangest places, even though no one seems to know how it got there! Just keeping the house somewhat hygienic can be a huge challenge, and the thought of having the house frequently invaded by visitors, or regularly adding more plates around the table, can overwhelm the average mother. So one of the questions I asked husbands was, "What are some ways you help your wife?"

One said he does not believe opening your home to outsiders on a regular basis is possible unless husbands are willing to pick up part of the load. "When our children were still young, I did almost all the vacuuming. Now that they are older, the children do this. I also washed most of the dishes. Our wives have a full plate with just fixing food and taking care of the children. So if families are going to open their homes, husbands need to get involved with the housework." Others spoke of asking visitors, especially those who visit frequently, to help.

We have had various foreign students in our home, and we have found they enjoy getting involved. Sometimes we ask them to fix meals, which provides a great opportunity to experience international cuisine right in our own home.

Several mothers shared how they prepare for the unexpected. Some keep frozen casseroles in the freezer, while others keep canned goods, soup, or other simple ingredients on hand so something can be quickly prepared if someone stops in. Giving a little thought to preparation can relieve the stress normally associated with unexpected guests. One of the comments I heard was the importance of simple meals. "People just want to spend time with a functioning family. Some have never seen one! They aren't coming for gourmet meals."

Another mother echoed a similar theme. "People are afraid their house or food won't be good enough. We have a very small living room, but that isn't a good excuse for not inviting people. If you want people to see Jesus, then just invite them into your small, modest setting. The carpet does not have to be clean, things don't have to match, and the meal doesn't have to be elaborate. Just show them what life is like in a Christian home." She went on to describe how even the noise and activities of children can be a blessing. "Don't put on a pretense. Just live your normal life, and the children will make them feel at home. They also get to see how much life, joy, and fulfillment a home can have without television."

It is easy to assume that the most effective way to develop rapport with neighbors is to give them things, and there is a time for this. During a sickness or after a catastrophe is an excellent time to deliver a meal, and God's people should be famous for this. But one of the most effective ways to build a relationship is to reveal a weakness or lack in your own life. Don't be afraid to borrow a tool or ask advice of your unbelieving neighbor. Allowing them to bless you in some way can be a powerful relationship builder, especially if you return the tool in a little better shape than when you borrowed it. Every person needs to feel valued. Too often we ply neighbors with gifts, hoping to gain their friendship. But this is rarely effective. If you can be humble enough to ask for help, this shows them that you value them as individuals. This can be powerful in causing them to feel accepted and helps build a stronger relationship.

A United Community Vision

Intentional hospitality works best when you have a church community that carries the same burden and has a united vision. I have spoken to many individuals who are afraid to take their co-workers to church for fear they won't be accepted. They are not sure how some church members would respond if their tattooed, body-pierced friend were to walk through the church doors on Sunday morning. Some who practice intentional hospitality feel very lonely within their congregation.

But I have also spoken with those who have experienced the opposite. One family told of a time when they were overwhelmed. They had struggling people staying in their home, they were trying to work with multiple relationship issues between people in their neighborhood, and they knew they weren't giving their children the time they needed. It was during this time they saw firsthand the blessing of a vibrant church community. "People in our congregation could see we were drowning, and they came alongside in a beautiful way. People brought meals and offered to help in various ways. We opened the mail one day to find an anonymous gift card to a local grocery store. There was a note attached that said, 'We know you are feeding a lot of people right now, and we wanted to help.'" Little gestures like this can help families who are being stretched feel supported and loved by their local congregation.

Maybe just reading this has made you tired. You are already busy, and adding something else sounds impossible. Or perhaps you have read through the warnings, problems, and potential challenges of inviting people from different religious, ethnic, or economic strata, and the effort seems too great. I don't know your situation, but I encourage you to lift these issues and potential challenges up before the Lord.

Life does have seasons, and if you have a houseful of young children or are caring for an elderly family member, you may be limited in your ability to reach out at this point in your life. On the other hand, if you are older and no longer have a busy household, you may be in a unique position to bless in ways that younger families can't. Many in our culture feel alienated and could use an older, experienced friend and voice in their lives.

One of the most challenging situations is living in a setting where others in your church do not carry the same burden. I have talked to families who feel they would be looked down on by their church community if they tried building relationships with their unbelieving neighbors. For them the social cost of obeying this teaching of Jesus looks almost insurmountable. Yet God never gives us a command without providing a way to obey, and there are many ways to build relationships without causing offense.

Regardless where you find yourself, purpose to use your home to bless others. Dilemmas will come, but rest assured, when you start caring about the stranger, the fatherless, and the widow, God will be there with you—because He cares about them too. And if you are fearful of what others will think when you begin associating with sinners—with people who aren't highly regarded by society—be of good cheer; you are in good company. Jesus was scorned for doing the same.[c]

---

[c] Matthew 9:10-13; Mark 2:15-17; Luke 5:27-32; Luke 7:34

Reaching America

CHAPTER 19

God: An Intentional Investor

J esus used many natural illustrations to describe spiritual truths to His followers. He said the kingdom of God resembles a seed cast on the ground,[a] a merchant who discovered a valuable pearl,[b] and a woman mixing leaven with flour.[c] He also used natural illustrations to reveal the character of God. The Lord is portrayed as a father forgiving his wayward son,[d] a bridegroom coming to receive His bride,[e] and

---

[a] Mark 4:26

[b] Matthew 13:45, 46

[c] Matthew 13:33

[d] Luke 15:11-32

[e] Matthew 25:1-13

a master who graciously forgives a servant who owes him a great debt.[f] Jesus was the master storyteller, and yet we understand these were not just stories. These parables shed light on critical questions that people had been pondering for centuries. They reveal truths about this powerful yet unseen God and disclose His nature and character.

But there is one account I believe we fail to give adequate attention to. It is a story that tells us so much about God and what He expects from us. It is commonly referred to as the parable of the talents. Jesus said the kingdom of heaven is like a rich man who entrusted his wealth to three managers before heading off on a journey.[g] He divided eight talents, or units of money, among three men, giving different amounts based on their management ability. Upon returning from his journey, he called them together and found these men had utilized different investment strategies. Two of them had gone out in the marketplace, done some trading, and doubled their assets. They had risked their master's money, yet they earned a good return on their investment. As any investor knows, doubling an asset requires risk. You cannot play safe and get a high rate of return. These two managers believed their lord wanted them to take a risk and invest aggressively. They believed hazard was preferable to hoarding.

But the other manager took a more conservative approach. He was fearful, believing it would be safer to cautiously protect the boss's assets and take as little risk as possible. So with furtive glances both ways to ensure no one was watching, he dug a hole and carefully buried the talent to await his master's return. He decided to play it safe, thinking he understood what his lord wanted. He believed his master was primarily concerned that nothing be lost.

[f] Matthew 18:23-35

[g] Matthew 25:14-30

Of course, we know the end of the story. The master returned, called these three men together, and asked for an account of their stewardship. The first two showed how they had doubled his assets, risking their boss's wealth by trading in order to profit in the end. They were thanked and rewarded. Then the third man came forward and explained his cautious approach. He told the master that he understood what kind of man he was, and explained in detail the great effort he expended to ensure his master would suffer no loss. And then comes the most incredible part of the story.

One would assume the master would show some measure of gratitude for the conservative manager. After all, he had not been negligent with his master's goods. He had not stolen the talent or used it for his own benefit. He had actually gone to great pains to safeguard that talent. But there was no word of commendation! No comment of affirmation or appreciation for the effort in carefully protecting what he had been given. The Bible says that the master lashed out in anger at this servant. "Thou wicked and slothful servant . . ."

What was this man actually guilty of? I would suggest his primary crime was not knowing the mind of his master.

Return on Investment

The master, representing God in this parable, expected return on his investment. He had expected his servants to put these talents to use. He was well aware there is risk in the marketplace, yet he desired more than just preservation. God gives us resources with the intent that we use them for His glory and for the furtherance and growth of His kingdom.

As I have considered the message in this parable, I have been sobered. All of my life I have been interested in identifying and pushing back against weak, insipid "Christianity" that constantly threatens the church. I have written against it, argued against it, and pushed back against the "easy believism" theology that relentlessly seems to creep into our circles. The church seems to constantly teeter on the edge of washout, almost ready to succumb to "the cares of this world, and the deceitfulness of riches, and the lusts of other things."[h] I have watched godly men become ensnared by wealth, churches absorbed into worldliness, and young people overwhelmed with electronic entertainment. Things seem to be flying apart, and my tendency is to pull in, avoid risk, and put my focus on preserving the blessings God has placed into my care. I have found myself imitating the third steward in this parable.

It is also possible to do this collectively, and I would suggest that we, as conservative Anabaptists, are in danger of forgetting the nature of our God. In the face of great risk and existential threats, it is easy to start thinking God's primary interest is to preserve—that the total definition of faithfulness is avoiding drift, and that God is most pleased when nothing is lost. Instead of being a group of truth-sharers, we become known as hole-diggers.

It is essential that we closely examine our concept of God and what He is trying to achieve here on earth. For when we see God incorrectly, strange anomalies occur. If God's primary concern is to preserve, then our attention will turn to size and depth of holes. We will spend all our time focusing on the effectiveness of holes of the past and even better methods of avoiding risk. But this parable of Jesus is clear. God expects us to produce return on His investment in our lives!

Understand, I am not saying we should cease being cautious about doctrinal error, live carelessly toward worldliness, or stop warning our people about the dangers of affluence. These are incredibly deceitful dangers and are a great threat to the church. We will need continual warning on these

---

[h] Mark 4:19

topics. If we fail to preserve the Biblical values we have been given, we will have nothing to share with others. This parable is not asking us to dispense with caution.

God expects us to produce return on His investment in our lives.

Investors understand there is a ratio, or balance, between risk and reward. A good investor takes active measures to avoid undue danger, and there are many examples where investors have failed to do this. As I look at the religious landscape, I am thankful that conservative Anabaptist churches have not forgotten the need for caution.

So how do we apply this parable today? We are left with two obvious questions that need to be answered in each age: First, what has God given us, in our day, to steward or manage? Second, what kind of return is God receiving on what He has invested?

What Have We Been Given?

Let's start with the first question. As I look at conservative Anabaptists, I see two obvious "talents" God has placed in our care. The first is a heritage of strong families. This is something we are known for. In a world where households seldom sit down together for meals and where solid, enduring marriages are almost a thing of the past, the Anabaptists shine. Divorce in our churches is almost unheard of, nurturing of children is promoted, and there is an abundance of families that enjoy being together. In fact, this is so normal in our communities that we fail to realize its rarity. Things are not perfect, but this is a tremendous blessing, a gift from God, and I would call it a "talent" He has placed in our hands.

The second area where we notably shine is in our occupational success and business acumen. The world observes this, and news articles by secular authors extol our work ethic and our ability to start and operate businesses. Some have made efforts to discover the "secret sauce," and books have been written purporting to share the hidden riddle of Anabaptist business success. Sometimes I hear people refer to this as "the German work ethic," but I believe it would be wiser to just acknowledge that this is another gift from God. None of us chose our ethnicity, our childhood training, or the culture we were born into. Business acumen, a good work ethic, management ability—call it what you wish—is another "talent" God has invested in our Anabaptist churches.

What Kind of Return Is God Receiving?

Now let's consider what kind of return on investment God is receiving in these two areas. Let's begin with our homes. We just looked at some families who are intentionally obeying the command of Jesus when forming their guest list. Yet, to be candid, these homes are the exception rather than the rule. Finding homes that have intentionally removed the bushel from their candle and frequently include their unbelieving neighbors or individuals from outside their social network are not as plentiful as we could wish. We tend to surround our dinner table with the very people Jesus said not to: our friends, our brethren, our relatives, and those who are able to invite us back to their home.[i] We even use the phrase, "It's our turn to have you," demonstrating that reciprocation is an expected social norm. I have been challenged as I realize the many ways I have protected "my" home, burying it if you will, and neglected to take the risk of following Jesus. Is this an area where God is receiving an unacceptable return on His investment?

What about our businesses? While gathering material for my book *It's Not Your Business,* I interviewed many business owners to learn more about the kingdom potential in conservative Anabaptist businesses.[20] Again, I found good examples of men who are purposefully using their businesses to demonstrate Jesus to a lost world. There are some businessmen who are intentionally using their companies to exhibit the kingdom

---

[i] Luke 14:12

Reaching America

of God here on earth. Some financially successful business owners are living very simple lives, enabling them to share with those in need. But I want to be clear. This is by no means universal, and there is much need for improvement. Too often, this is another talent that is being buried. There are so many ways our businesses could demonstrate Jesus here in America. Further, far too much wealth is being squandered in selfish pursuits. We have many business owners who have not yet grasped the great potential for the kingdom that is slipping through their fingers, and much of their income is being wasted on expensive vacations, hobbies, and extravagant housing. Our businesses have been incredibly blessed and contain so much kingdom potential! God has poured, and continues to pour, this financial blessing into our lives, and I'm afraid we forget that He is expecting a return on His investment!

Our homes and our businesses—two areas where God has invested heavily within the conservative Anabaptist communities. So why do we struggle to lay these on the altar? Why aren't we utilizing these for the kingdom as we could or should? There could be many answers to these questions. It might simply be due to selfishness. We like to gather with people of similar backgrounds, ethnicity, and economic status. We enjoy spending the income derived from "our" business to make our houses nicer, our lives more pleasant, or our vacations more enjoyable. As you analyze your life, be honest. Maybe selfishness is part of the problem.

But I suspect there is another reason. I believe most of us really want to reach out. I suspect you wouldn't have read this far if you didn't care about your neighbor. I would propose we often neglect to fully utilize what God has given us for the same reason the third manager in Jesus' parable dug a hole. We are fearful of failure.

We reason that if we actually operated our businesses as Jesus said, our income might be affected. We might even lose our farm or business. There is the possibility we might lose more than we gain. When we think of opening our homes, it is the same story. Associating with those from a different background can be a little scary, and inviting them into our homes could present some awkward situations. So instead of launching out in faith, we succumb to fear. We take the valuable investment God has placed in our care, sneak out fearfully with a shovel, and bury these "talents."

There is also another fear that many of us struggle with. As mentioned earlier, our world has changed dramatically. Not everyone has been raised to see the beauty in the Judeo-Christian worldview. Many in America today do not appreciate or value the Bible. Standards have changed, and we have difficulty knowing how to relate to people who don't share our worldview. I enjoy dialogue with people who share my perspectives and cultural background. But how do I talk about spiritual issues with someone who believes that the Bible is just an outdated book of fairy tales? And what if he presents scientific evidence I have never thought of or am unable to refute? What if she asks a question I can't answer? What if they present evidence that makes my belief system look foolish?

These are all questions I have wrestled with. I have had some embarrassing moments and been in discussions with unbelievers where I didn't do a very good job of defending Christianity. Sometimes out of fear, we shrink back from engaging those we meet. So, knowing my own limitations with answering difficult religious questions, and knowing that many others carry these same fears, I went in search of answers. In this next section, we are going to "listen in" as seasoned men respond to the world's hard questions. Hopefully this will be as helpful to you as it has been to me.

Part Four

LEARNING FROM EXPERIENCE

CHAPTER 20

"Hello, I Have a Question..."

I n the past fifty years, the religious landscape has changed dramatically. I grew up in the country, and our family had good relationships with all our neighbors. While most of them were not strong believers, all of them had a basic foundational understanding and belief in God. They might not have attended church regularly, yet I knew they had respect for us, our church, and our way of life. To my knowledge, none of our neighbors professed being an atheist or an agnostic. There was a basic understanding that God existed, and a certain moral framework seemed to be understood and accepted. If my father wanted to have a discussion with one of them regarding morality or ethics, he had a place to start.

Our world today is different. With the rise of postmodernism and a general suspicion about anything absolute, there is often little foundation for meaningful discussion. The ideology of "that may be true for you, but it isn't for me" is being promoted everywhere—from universities to coffee shops. The message is subtle but powerful. Many people are also being indoctrinated by constant exposure to the entertainment world. There are multiple ways to have endless electronic entertainment delivered directly to your device, and the music being listened to and the movies being watched are saturated with postmodern philosophy. If you keep ingesting this material long enough, your morals will shift. You will conclude that the most important issue is your own happiness. You will learn that there are no absolutes, and that nothing is as important as having your own way. All this, of course, flies in the face of Biblical truth, and soon the Bible begins to sound strange and stuffy. People wonder why an outdated book like that should dictate their choices. Many are just checking out of religion.

The Nones, addressed earlier, are the fastest growing religious sector in America. In a 2019 study, they represented 23.1 percent of the population. That is up from 21.6 percent in 2016 and is now roughly the same as those who identify themselves as Catholic. During this time, those claiming to be evangelical dropped from 23.9 percent in 2016 to 22.5 percent in 2019.[21] This means there are now more Nones in America than evangelical Christians. This is a huge cultural shift, and with it come some challenges. How do you start a conversation with someone who does not believe God even exists? If there is no underlying basis for belief, how can you discuss anything? How are we to have meaningful dialogue? Who makes the call regarding gay marriage or any of the various gender issues our culture faces?

> How do you start a conversation with someone who does not believe God even exists?

I have talked to people on airplanes whose lives and worldviews were so far from God that

I did not know where to start. And sometimes, to my own shame, I have been so unsure that I just turned back to the book I was reading, fearful of doing more harm than good. Their perception of Christianity is so marred that I am afraid pointed statements or even direct questions will simply reinforce a wrong perception of God.

With a desire to learn from men with more experience, I have investigated the responses of the men who answer the phone each day with Christian Aid Ministries' Billboard Evangelism program. For the last several years I have been reviewing their phone conversations, trying to learn from their knowledge. Each morning I received transcripts from their conversations and tried to gain insight.

I wanted to gain a better understanding of our culture in America and what the religious terrain looks like. What kind of questions are Americans asking? What are their main concerns, and what do they believe? I also wanted to learn how to respond to difficult questions. The men answering the phone each day are seasoned followers of Jesus. They have had opportunity to see what kind of responses are effective. When they answer the phone, they need to be grounded in the Word and need to be capable of answering a wide range of questions. They must also be able to respond with both truth and grace.

In the next chapter we will take a look at some of these calls.

CHAPTER 21

Listening In

"How do people in America think?" we sometimes ask. "What are their concerns and what questions do they have?" As we have noted before, times have changed and are changing, and it is often hard to really understand the views and values of society around us.

This chapter will give us a taste of the many calls Christian Aid Ministries' Billboard Evangelism program receives each day. I have tried to select calls that might be helpful to the reader both in understanding our culture and in learning how to respond. The calls are categorized into six basic categories, but there is some overlap since some callers discuss more than one topic. For readers who would like to learn more about responding to questions like this, there are additional calls in the Appendix at the back of this book.

When referring to the caller I have used fictitious names, and I have identified the Phone Team Member answering the call as the PTM.

1. Atheists and Agnostics

Although atheists and agnostics have similar beliefs, there is some difference. An atheist is one who has made up his mind. He believes he has a good grasp of the facts and has concluded that no god—or God—exists. An agnostic, on the other hand, has not made a final decision. While he may enjoy discussing the possibilities and arguing about the nature or existence of God, he is not sure we can ascertain anything regarding God's existence. He is taking the relatively comfortable position of not being sure; therefore he has nothing to defend.

Victoria

Victoria: "Hello, will you lead me in a prayer?"

PTM: "I can. But before I do that, could you tell me a little about yourself, your experience, and your walk with the Lord? Are you prepared to meet God?"

Victoria: "Well, I currently don't believe in God, but I'm open to it."

PTM: "Did you grow up in a Christian home?"

Victoria: "No."

PTM: "Do you know much about the Bible?"

Victoria: "No, I have never read the Bible."

The team member then told Victoria his own story, how he had been raised in a Christian home, came to faith in Christ, committed his life to Him, and shared how the blood of Jesus has forgiven him of his sins. This confused Victoria, and she wondered what blood had to do with all of this. So the PTM explained that there had to be a sacrifice for sin and that Jesus Christ was willing to die for us. Jesus, as God in the flesh, was sinless, and through His death we can be forgiven and be given new life.

Victoria: "So, do you still sin?

PTM: "I do at times, even though I have been forgiven for my past sins."

Victoria: "Give me an example."

PTM: "Well, maybe I'm stressed out about something, get upset with my wife, and say something to her that I shouldn't. Later on I realize what I have done, so I go back to my wife and apologize."

Victoria: "You mean getting angry is sin?"

PTM: "Yes, it can be."

Victoria: "So, what do you think about homosexuality?"

PTM: "It is a sin just like other sins."

Victoria: "Well, are all sins the same in God's sight?"

PTM: "All sin separates from God, but not all sins have the same results. For example, being angry with a man and killing him are both sins. But the results are different."

Victoria: "What if you live in sin completely, but go to church every Sunday and believe in God?"

PTM: "Well, just because someone goes to church doesn't mean they're godly or Christians. If you're born again and committed to following Jesus, then you're not going to be sinning. But just because you go to church does not make you right with God. There are a lot of people who go to church who are not going to be in heaven."

This conversation continued for a long time as Victoria tried to understand what it actually means to be a Christian. They covered topics ranging from how old a person is when they become accountable before God, to whether a murderer can actually be forgiven, to the second coming of Jesus. Victoria seemed to have picked up bits and pieces of information about Christianity but had never had the opportunity to ask the many questions swirling around in her mind.

Max

The message had said "Jesus is Alive," and this had pushed Max over the edge. He had been a Christian years ago, but after attending college, studying the history of the church, and seeing the ruthless way "Christian" nations like Germany treated human beings, he walked away from God. Now he considers himself an atheist. Max spoke knowledgably about both science and Biblical texts. He has read the Bible through many times but has concluded we should live by reasonable deduction rather than ancient texts.

Max was especially bitter toward certain Christian teachers who promote a prosperity gospel and take advantage of people financially.

> PTM: "Max, you have spent a good deal of time talking about the problems with Christianity, but what has atheism brought to this world?"
>
> Max: "We don't know yet because atheism hasn't had a chance."
>
> PTM: "Explain what you mean."
>
> Max: "Those in power haven't allowed us to try it. At every turn, it is put down when anyone tries to go public with it, so people are forced to stifle their feelings about the fact God doesn't exist."
>
> PTM: "Why do you think true Christians throughout history

have been willing to suffer for what they stood for, but atheists have not?"

Max: "Well, for the first few hundred years, Christians were very careful and didn't get too radical with their beliefs."

PTM: "But Max, what about the account of Stephen in the book of Acts? And how about men like the Apostle Paul, who was beheaded for his faith? He didn't seem to be very cautious. And then there is the record of those first twelve apostles. All but one of them were martyred for their faith. Those men, if anyone would have, knew that Christianity was true. And if it was a false narrative, they certainly wouldn't have died for it."

Max: "I guess the thing that bothers me the most are some of the teachings in the Bible, and the hypocrisy in Christianity. The book of Leviticus is just a handbook for torturing animals, and I am strongly opposed to cruelty to animals. And I have seen so much insincerity in Christianity!"

PTM: "So, Max, what do you think we should do?"

Max: "I think we should spend our time on earth practicing some of the things Jesus taught, but we shouldn't worship a God who allows hell. I don't think we will ever figure everything out. But eventually mankind will destroy this planet, and mankind will be extinct. It may be a few years from now or several hundred, but eventually everything will stop."

PTM: "That is a very bleak picture, Max. As I read my Bible, I see a God who loves us, who wants to bless us, and who ultimately will make every wrong right. But if I accept your way of looking at life, what are we to live for?"

Max: "Why does there have to be a purpose for us to live for?"

2. Struggling or Facing a Crisis

Our Western society has become a melting pot of religious confusion. Having thrown off all absolutes, millions are casting about in search of a cause or crusade they can join to give meaning to life. Whether it's fighting climate change, following health fads, or saving the whales, many are on a quest for meaning. Others simply succumb to being entertained, distracting themselves by following sports teams, listening to music, or watching funny sitcoms or the latest movie. But underneath all this is a deep sense of emptiness. People can surround themselves with diversions, but occasionally a crisis hits that is painful enough to penetrate the façade. Many people who call after seeing a billboard are confused or discouraged; some are in the middle of a crisis.

> Our Western society has become a melting pot of religious confusion.

Harvey

Some callers call repeatedly. They may be struggling with a particular weakness or obsession, or just with basic unbelief. They call searching for someone or something to help them deal with life. Harvey is one of these, and he struggles with feeling forgiven by God.

> Harvey: "So what does it take to be forgiven by God?"
>
> PTM: "God will not despise someone who comes to Him with a broken spirit. The Bible says, 'A broken and a contrite heart, O God, thou wilt not despise.' "[a]
>
> Harvey: "So how often can a man repent and still be forgiven?"
>
> PTM: "A person initially becomes a Christian when he repents

---

[a] Psalm 51:17

of his past sinful life, receives Jesus as the Lord of his life, is baptized, and receives the gift of the Holy Spirit.[b] But then he lives in constant repentance of anything that comes to his attention that is not in obedience to Jesus. By this process of repentance and change, Jesus is able to make us more and more into His image by the power of the Holy Spirit.[c] Are you a follower of Jesus?"

Harvey: "I am not, but I have led many people to God. Seventeen years ago I was sexually abused and became a victim. My body was defiled, and I can't ever be acceptable to God again."

PTM: "Any person can be victimized, but he will not become a victim unless he allows the victimization to define him. A victim lives a life of blaming others and making excuses for his situation. But a victimized person can choose to be a victor by forgiving the victimizer and moving on with his life of walking with Jesus."

Harvey: "I was a Christian when this happened. I knew what it was to feel the presence of God. That feeling left when I was victimized, and I have never been able to get it back."

PTM: "You are allowing yourself to become trapped as you focus on your feelings. The Gospel focuses on actions. When it says 'love your enemies,' it doesn't describe feelings. It tells us to bless our enemies, pray for them, and do good to them. These are actions, not feelings. The proof that a man has the Holy Spirit is not just a feeling, but the fact that he is led by the Spirit."[d]

---

[b] Acts 2:38

[c] 2 Corinthians 3:18

[d] Romans 8:14

This conversation lasted almost an hour, and as they continued it became evident that Harvey was very bitter toward his victimizer, as well as God, for what had happened to him. The PTM urged him to ask for God's help to forgive the victimizer and to trust God in gratitude for the forgiveness and love He provides. Harvey said he lives in terror, and believes he is a hopeless reprobate going to hell. He is so fearful that he drinks each night so he can sleep.

Sophia

It has been eight years since Sophia's son was murdered, and she still struggles to understand why God was not there when she needed Him.

> Sophia: "I know I need God. I don't know how atheists do it. But I don't know how I can trust Jesus. I don't understand why God took my son and has been silent about it for years!"
>
> PTM: "I lost a family member twelve years ago and I understand the anguish you are going through. But my loss has actually strengthened my faith in God. In the seventh chapter of Matthew, Jesus promises us that if we build our life on the teachings of Jesus, the storms that are sure to come will not destroy us. Our faith in Jesus helps us weather the test."
>
> Sophia: "But why doesn't God speak and let me know why all this happened?"
>
> PTM: "God tests us at times by being silent. Through such experiences of silence our faith can be tested severely. God has always tested people this way. Job was a man who was severely tested. But after he was tested, God revealed Himself to him. Sophia, if you can stand true to God even with all your doubts, I believe God will reveal Himself to you."

3. Creation versus Evolution

The subject of origins has been a major topic of discussion for years. How did this universe with all its complexity and diversity come into existence? There was a time when the majority of people in America believed that God created the earth and humans. But that has changed. Fewer than half now believe that God created man in his present form within approximately the past 10,000 years.[22] So as you reach out to your neighbors, or the man in the supermarket, you cannot assume he believes the Biblical narrative. The same is true for those who see billboards and call with questions.

Michael

The tone of voice can tell a lot about a caller, and there was a bit of arrogance in this one's voice.

> Michael: "I want to put up a billboard promoting evolution!"
>
> PTM: "Well, you can certainly do that. What you need to do is to contact the people who have the billboard frames, negotiate with them, and tell them what you want. You can do that, just the same as we do."
>
> Michael: "So, I take it that you people don't believe in evolution."
>
> PTM: "Well, if you're talking about microevolution—we don't have any problem with that at all. As you know, we have cabbage, cauliflower, kohlrabi, and Brussels sprouts, and all of these come from the same original plant. They have the same DNA. The only difference is that we have bred them into different plants. It is the same DNA, but we have just bred it to do different things. Of course, macroevolution is an entirely different issue. A cabbage will never become an orange or an oak tree; it will always remain in the same family. Animals are the

same. Through intensive breeding, dogs can be bred to look very different. But they will never become anything other than a dog."

Michael: "But don't you think it's short-sighted to say that a eucalyptus tree could never become an orange tree?"

PTM: "No, that isn't short-sighted at all; it's how it is. The fossil record and our current understanding of eucalyptus trees and orange trees show us that they're not the same and never will be the same, regardless how much time you give them."

Michael: "I have never heard it explained like that."

PTM: "I was talking to a doctor one time who was a believer, and I asked him how he came to believe in God. He said. 'When I was in med school I was studying genetics. And as I was studying DNA, I began to notice that what I was seeing under the microscope and what I was being told by my lecturers were two different things. DNA is far too complex to have arranged itself. There is a design, and where there is a design there must be a designer.' This doctor concluded by saying, 'I began searching for answers, and I found God.' "

Michael: "Okay, well, thank you for a friendly conversation."

Emily

This young lady is a scientist, and she called because she is searching for answers to the question of origins. Emily grew up in a home where atheism was taught and assumed. Today she is open to the possibility that there might be a God. In her own words, she is "exploring God, godliness, and Christianity." Emily wanted to know if a person is required to believe in a literal six-day creation to believe in the Bible or be a Christian.

PTM: "There are Christians who believe in an old earth and others who believe in a young earth. Those who believe in a young earth generally believe that creation was completed in six literal days. I personally believe the world was created in six days. Moses in the book of Exodus says, 'For in six days the LORD made heaven and earth, the sea, and all that in them is, and rested the seventh day:' "[e]

Emily: "Okay, that is helpful."

PTM: "So, Emily, I am curious. You said that your home was atheistic. What has caused you to start thinking about God and exploring the possibility of His existence?"

Emily: "I am a scientist, and I believe in evolution—and it makes sense to me. But where did the first person come from and how did life begin? You have to have something to produce that first atom. It seems obvious that it has to be something outside of itself, outside of the universe and outside of natural evolution. That is what makes me think there must be something out there, and that is why I am exploring the possibility of God."

4. From Curious to Serious

Our culture has moved toward a foundational belief that science, rather than the Bible, has the answers for our lives. Many have grown up in homes where education, technology, and new scientific development are being touted as the cure for the ailments of society. "Just give science enough time," they say, "and continued research will take care of everything." While those of us who believe in the truth of Scripture are

---

[e] Exodus 20:11

troubled by this cultural shift, there is a corresponding upside. Science encourages continued investigation and promotes continual research. As a result, people are on a quest for more information. Some may just be curious, but others have good questions and are serious seekers.

Hunter

Hunter called with questions regarding origins, evolution, and whether there really is a need for an intelligent Creator. Then he had questions about the Bible.

> Hunter: "I don't understand why the Bible has to prohibit pre-marital and extramarital sex. Why does that even matter? If people consent to be involved in sexual activity outside of marriage, why should anyone else care?"

> PTM: "Sex was provided to allow humans to procreate. However, there is another very important reason it was given. We are designed to have a relationship with others, and intimacy in marriage is intended to enhance relational bonding between a husband and wife. But outside of marriage it can do just the opposite, creating distrust, deep hurt, and painful betrayal. A girl in such a relationship hopes for a commitment of love in return, but if the boy has no intention of committing to her, she is betrayed. This is a great injustice. In addition, living this way weakens the basis for trust after marriage. Just by observation we can see that God's way is only reasonable."

> Hunter: "Okay, but what about lying? Why should it matter if a person doesn't always tell the truth? Everyone has to stretch the truth a little in difficult situations. Why does the Bible have to get involved in this?"

> PTM: "Truth is foundational for any human relationship to thrive, and trust is impossible without truth. Truth is essential, and God's law is realistic when it lists lying as a sin."

Hunter: "I have a friend who was recently killed in a car accident. He wasn't walking with Jesus, so how will God judge him?"

PTM: "Only God knows what your friend was doing with the truth that he knew. That's why we are not to judge. These are difficult circumstances and we just trust these situations to a God who is both just and merciful. It is important to remember that God's desire is more than just getting people to heaven. He also wants to bring redemption to the world we live in. He wants peace, justice, and love to control our lives and society."

Hunter: "Thank you for that perspective. I actually was a follower of Jesus at one time. But I stopped because my morality didn't mesh with the Gospel. So I found a faith that allowed for my moral choices."

PTM: "Well, I would encourage you to study the Gospels and reconsider that Jesus' way actually gives us an authentic humanity. All other ways will ultimately lead to disappointment and destruction. Jesus said one time, 'These things have I spoken unto you, that my joy might remain in you, and that your joy might be full.'ᶠ His teachings were not given to make our life miserable. Rather, they were provided by our Creator Himself to help us live to our maximum potential!"

Nora

"What is the meaning of the billboard message 'There IS Evidence for GOD'?" The woman was angry, talking vehemently, and a little difficult to understand. "My husband and I are driving and we just

---

ᶠ John 15:11

saw your billboard with the picture of a baby on it. I'm black and my husband is white. Recently someone made fun of our mixed-race marriage. So I want to know. What are the implications if we have a child?"

There was silence for a moment as the PTM wasn't sure what she was driving at. But before he could ask for clarification, Nora continued, "One of my fellow church members recently implied that God's blessing cannot rest on a child from a mixed-race marriage. So we want to know what you think."

> PTM: "Well, Nora, my wife and I are Caucasian, but we have one black and three biracial grandchildren by adoption. To us they are extremely precious and perfect, and we love them dearly. We don't think of them any differently than our biological grandchildren. The Bible says that we are all of one blood, and therefore racism is wrong."
>
> Nora: "You really believe that?"
>
> PTM: "Absolutely! The only difference is the pigmentation of the skin. We are all of equal value. If God should grant you a child, that child would be perfect, crafted by the hand of God. Your child would be just as special and have just as much purpose as any other child ever born. If you desire children, go ahead and bear children—then rejoice in the perfection of the handiwork of God! And God bless you."

There was a short silence, then Nora replied, "Oh, that is the most wonderful thing I have ever heard. You have absolutely made my day!"

Jaxon

Jaxon grew up in an unreligious home, so he knew little about God or the Bible, but he wanted to learn. The PTM began by describing the Bible, beginning in Genesis and continuing through the Old and New

Testaments. Someone at college had given Jaxon a New Testament, but he hadn't read it yet. They spent some time discussing sin, what it is, and how to deal with it. Jaxon began to confess some sins in his life.

> Jaxon: "I have had sexual relations with my stepmother, and that bothers me."

> PTM: "Jaxon, you need to confess that to God, along with any other sins you have committed."

> Jaxon: "Do you think I should confess to my father?"

> PTM: "Yes, I think you should."

> Jaxon: "I am willing to do that, but what about stealing?"

> PTM: "What do you mean?"

> Jaxon: "Well, I stole something pretty valuable from my brother several years ago. My brother reported it to the police, but no one ever discovered that I was the thief. I sold the stolen item and then used the funds to pay for my college tuition. Now I am about to graduate, and if I tell my brother what actually happened, I will probably go to jail. So I am just wondering, would it be okay to just confess it to God?"

> PTM: "No, you should go ahead and confess it to your brother. That would be the right thing. Then you can offer to make it right and repay him. But if you have to go to jail, you should accept the consequences of your sin. This is much better than keeping sin hidden."

> Jaxon: "Wow, I am going to need to think about this. I think I should start by taking your suggestion and reading the book of Matthew first. Could I call you after I finish it so we can talk more?"

5. Morality Issues

One of the remarkable evidences for the existence of God is the universal presence of morality in humanity. Every human seems to know inherently that certain behaviors are good, while others are inappropriate. For example, regardless where you live on the globe, everyone seems to agree that an adult stealing food from a small child, or randomly murdering someone, is wrong. Animals may not grasp this, but humans do. Morals seem to be intrinsically part of being human, and yet our culture is attempting to ignore this reality.

> Morals seem to be intrinsically part of being human, and yet our culture is attempting to ignore this reality.

Relativism, the belief that truth and morality are not absolute, is prevalent today. Moral absolutes, and especially Biblical absolutes, are out of favor. This has affected how Americans think about sexual morality, divorce and remarriage, homosexuality, and gender issues. Many calls come in asking questions about what the Bible has to say on these issues. Some are seriously seeking truth, while others despise any moral reference point outside of themselves.

Jacob

The first question Jacob asked was, "How does God feel about gays?"

The PTM took him to several Scriptures that speak of homosexuality,[g] and then Jacob had another question. "Is it fair that God would make a person with a desire and not allow him to fulfill it?"

> PTM: "It's not a matter of fairness, but of right and wrong. For example, I am married to a wonderful woman, but I am

---

[g] 1 Corinthians 6:9; Romans 1:24-28

a normal man and when I see certain things I face the temptation to be unfaithful to my wife. Is that fair? I have that kind of appetite, but God calls unfaithfulness to my wife adultery and condemns it. He is the lawgiver. He made us, owns us, and I get my sense of right and wrong from the Scriptures. He has outlined the boundaries for intimate relationship since the beginning as one man and one woman married for life."

Jacob: "So what does God think of the fact that you hate gay people?"

PTM: "It is not a matter of hatred but of truth. I love gay people, and God loves gay people. The Bible says that even while we were sinners, Christ died for us.[h] God loves all men and women, but He hates sin, regardless which sin it is."

Jacob seemed to appreciate this response and wanted more time to think about this. The PTM pleaded with him to search the Scriptures to discover what God has to say on this topic, rather than listening to our culture. He also recommended the booklet *Is God Anti-Gay?*[23] and Jacob said he would read it.

Ellie

The voice on the phone was that of a young girl. "Hello, I discovered that I'm gay. Does God hate me?"

PTM: "No, the Bible says that God loves all men and women everywhere."

Ellie: "Well, my mother told me that I'm going to hell, and that she hates me. I also discovered that I'm a boy. Is it okay to be transgender?"

---

[h] Romans 5:8

PTM: "Ellie, the Bible says that God made mankind male and female, and I believe God made us how He wanted us to be. Have you tried talking to a pastor?"

Ellie: "My pastor told me that God loves me just the way I am, but now my pastor died, so I'm not sure who to talk to."

PTM: "Well, Ellie, I don't know a lot about your situation, but I would encourage you to accept the way God made you. Spend some time praying about it, and it might be good to get some professional help."

Ellie broke down and cried at this point. The PTM could hear her sobbing on the other end of the line. Finally she spoke. "Well, biologically I am a girl, so I'll pray to God and ask Him to help me, and to guide me in getting the help I need."

Emma

Emma had seen a billboard, and wanted an interview for her school project. She began asking a series of questions, including, "Are you a devout Christian?" and, "Did you vote for Donald Trump?"

The PTM told Emma that he hadn't voted for anyone, and that he isn't political. Emma didn't know what to think about this. So the PTM told her that instead of going to the polls, he votes direct—he prays. So Emma wanted to know who he is praying for in the next election and what he thought about abortion. When the PTM told her he loved life more than death, Emma began sharing some scenarios of very difficult situations, attempting to prove that there are times when an abortion is warranted.

PTM: "Those are interesting scenarios, but would you like for me to share a real story?"

Emma: "But some of those were real. But tell me yours."

PTM: "We had a young mother in our congregation who was

pregnant, and her doctor insisted she needed an abortion. He told her if she started into labor she would hemorrhage and die. This mother was opposed to abortion and refused to follow the doctor's advice. When the time got close for the baby to be born, we had an anointing service and prayed over her as the Bible teaches. A little ahead of her due date, they did a C-section, and even though it wasn't easy, the baby and mother were both fine. That little girl is eleven years old now, and as she goes bouncing down our church aisle each Sunday, I am always glad the mother made the choice she did!"

Emma: "That is great, but I can give you other scenarios where it didn't work out like that."

PTM: "Well, Emma, you know, either you're pro-life or you're pro-death. God has given life, and only God has the right to take life."

This discussion went on for some time, and Emma finally began to tell a little of her past. She had been raised by two lesbian mothers and asked if the PTM considered himself a feminist.

PTM: "I'm not a feminist, but I'm not the opposite of that either. We have a very good marriage, and I appreciate and value my wife. God intended that men love their wives, and I love mine. She has been a tremendous blessing to my life!"

Emma: "Am I an illegitimate child because I was born of one of the two mamas?"

PTM: "Well, it certainly is not God's design."

Emma: "So you are saying I'm not God's design?"

PTM: "That's not what I said. What I am saying is that the situation into which you were born is not God's design."

Emma: "So if you had a child that turned out to be homosexual, how would you treat that child?"

PTM: "With love and kindness."

Emma: "Would you try to change them?"

PTM: "I would present the truth to them, because only the truth will make you free."

At every turn in the conversation it became clearer that Emma was very much against Christianity. The PTM tried to point her back to truth very calmly, but at the conclusion of their conversation, Emma suddenly cursed God with the vilest of curses, repeating these profanities over and over several times before abruptly hanging up.

6. Religious Confusion

Many around us today are perplexed and have questions about religion. Some profess Christianity yet carry erroneous doctrines. Others seem genuinely confused and are unsure how to respond to the seemingly endless proliferation of religious groups. Still others are mystified by the multitude of spiritual leaders in our world, each insisting that they have the correct understanding of truth. In the past, people grew up and lived out their lives in one setting, possibly never being exposed to another religion or worldview. But today, through travel and technology, the average citizen is exposed to differing perspectives. So when they see a phone number on a billboard saying that truth is available, many call.

Harrison

Harrison called asking if we believe Jesus was a prophet, and the PTM replied that we do.i He then wanted to know if there are any prophets living today.

---

[i] Deuteronomy 18:15; Acts 3:22. Although we believe that Jesus was much more than a prophet, Scripture does refer to Him this way.

PTM: "The Bible says that in the past God spoke to us through His prophets, but in these last days He has spoken by His Son.[j] Jesus is the final revelation and the Apostle Paul says that anyone giving a different message should be accursed."[k]

Harrison: "Well, the Mormons have been visiting me, and I have been considering some of the things they have shared. What do you think about their teachings?"

PTM: "Joseph Smith claimed that the Christian church was in apostasy until he updated the Gospels. This was an extremely arrogant claim, and he injected all kinds of false teachings such as the possibility that we can become gods with our own universes in the next life. One of his revelations was that blacks could not be a part of the Mormon priesthood. Of course, when race became an issue in the United States in the 1970s, the Mormons got a new revelation that blacks could now be part of the priesthood. I could never trust such contradictory revelations. I know they told you if you pray you will receive a burning in your heart that would prove that the Book of Mormon is true, but nowhere in the Scriptures are we told that we are to test truth by a burning in our heart."

Harrison: "They have actually set a date now for my baptism, but I haven't been sure that I should go through with it."

PTM: "Harrison, I would really warn you against that. Before you go any further down that road I would encourage you to listen to a message called *Why People Leave LDS.*"[24]

Harrison: "I have been skeptical about the weird things the Mormons believe, but I have found them to be such nice people."

---

[j] Hebrews 1:1, 2

[k] Galatians 1:8, 9

Hasan

The billboard had proclaimed that God had created this world in the beginning, and Hasan called to let us know he appreciated the message. He believes evolution is wrong and it bothers him that so many people subscribe to this lie. Hasan is a Muslim and seemed to be a very committed one. He does not believe Jesus actually died on the cross, but believes God just took Him up to heaven. Hasan was very vocal about the faults of Christians. They don't live holy lives like Muslims do, he said. Good Muslims bow with their heads to the ground like Jesus did, their ladies cover their heads and dress modestly, and they don't practice fornication. Good Muslims don't drink alcohol or eat pork either, but Christians do all these things.

When Hasan was finished with his rant against Christianity, the PTM responded. "Hasan, it might surprise you to know that the wives of the men who answer the calls in this ministry cover their heads. All our wives do this. We also don't practice fornication or get drunk. In fact, we teach against this."

This was a shock to Hasan. The PTM then responded to some of the other statements Hasan had made. "The idea that Jesus didn't actually die is not supported historically. No one believed that before Muhammed, and I would encourage you to investigate further."

But Hasan didn't seem to see a need for more investigation. "When you're on the right path, you don't need to examine it."

The dialogue had to end because it was time for Hasan to pray. But in spite of Hasan's confidence, the PTM ended the conversation feeling that some seeds had been planted.

CHAPTER 22

Lessons Learned

"Listening in" as phone team members have responded to various questions has probably sparked many thoughts. Some of the answers may have intrigued you, and others you might have worded differently. We all have different gifts, perspectives, and past experiences. All this has a huge impact on how we respond to questions from individuals who are seeking, or reacting to, the truth.

As a young man I had definite opinions on the subject of outreach. I firmly believed I possessed truth, was certain some others did not, and as a new believer I felt an obligation to share the Gospel with those I came in contact with. In many ways my motives were good, and yet looking back there was an important ingredient lacking in many of my encounters: humility.

I remember sitting beside a man on a plane and trying to engage him in conversation. I had not flown by myself very often and saw this as an excellent opportunity. I began by trying to get a friendly conversation going. I asked questions about his family and his job but got no results. It was like going to the well and pumping an old hand pump with no results—nothing but air. Finally the man put down his book, turned to me very deliberately, and started asking questions. Within about ten minutes I felt as if I had walked into a meat grinder.

This man had grown up in a Christian home and had walked away from faith. He saw Christianity as a waste of time and was much better prepared than I was for a religious debate. He asked me about my faith and wondered why I still believed in an ancient, self-contradicting book like the Bible. He compared the Bible with other ancient writings (many of which I had never heard of), explaining why they were superior, and then, like icing on a cake, showered me with all kinds of "facts" and statistics proving the validity of evolution. And he did it all so kindly!

I meekly got off that plane like a whipped puppy. I had taken my seat with subtle self-confidence that I was ready to give an answer for my faith. But I disembarked with a fresh dose of much-needed humility. My proverbial tail was between my legs.

Maybe you have had similar experiences. We want to share the blessing of the Gospel with others, but we are not always sure how, and sometimes we do a poor job. Consequently, it has blessed me to have the opportunity to observe and learn from these men who answer the billboard calls. In this chapter I want to summarize some observations and basic lessons I have learned, both from them and from personal experience.

1. *Seek to understand before attempting to be understood.* Looking back, I had a greater desire to tell people than to listen and understand where they were coming from. If I had first taken

time to understand the man on that plane, things might have ended up differently. Remember, everyone has a story that is of value to them. It is important that we listen, learn, and understand before trying to teach. Empathize with their struggles. Let them know you care, and weep with them that weep.[a]

2. *Respect human dignity.* Every person has been created in the image of God, and this fact alone gives each one value. Respecting their dignity means being careful how fast we push into their lives without permission. Forcing someone to listen to the "Gospel message" because he happens to be strapped in the airplane seat beside me is not respecting him as a human. There is a time to speak truth into people's lives, even difficult truths they don't want to hear, but we need to be very careful. Pushing them to make an instant decision on our first encounter may cause them to feel like they have little value. They may also sense you are being driven more by a desire to save their souls (another win on your soul-saving scorecard) than by a genuine love for them. It is essential that we prayerfully analyze our motives.

3. *Learn to ask good questions.* This one is still hard for me. Too often I assume I should have an immediate answer for every question. But one of the reasons unchurched people flee Christians is because they feel shut down and unheard, and a good question allows them to feel heard. When we respond to every question with a snappy cliché or canned answer, they instinctively sense we're giving little real thought to their question. Asking good questions in return conveys the thought that we really care, and this can often be more

---

[a] Romans 12:15

effective than immediate answers. When people speak of difficulties in their lives, ask them to tell you more. Allow them the opportunity to explore their own feelings. Many times Jesus responded to a hard question with one of His own, and this can be a powerful tool.

4. *Don't try to hit a homerun.* I noticed that each phone team member operates a little differently. Some are more aggressive with their questions and others take a softer approach. But one thing impressed me. All seemed content with small movements. When we go out determined to move people in a dramatic way in a short time, we almost always do damage. God can move people dramatically, and He still does! But we should be content with small movements, as long as they are moving in the right direction. If you are dealing with an avowed atheist, just getting him to question his assumptions is huge. When working with a Christian who has never really given much thought to actually applying the Sermon on the Mount, just leaving him with a vision of the impact a kingdom community could have on our world can be transformative. Start where they are, and with God's help move them a little closer to His kingdom.

5. *Be transparent about your own uncertainties.* This may seem counterintuitive, but few things move a hardened atheist like a Christian admitting that there are things he also does not understand about God. Be willing at times to share your struggles in understanding why God allows things like pain and suffering. Let them know there are things that do not always make sense to you either. But don't stop there. If you are a follower of Jesus, you have also found reasons to trust God in the middle of your questions. Be transparent about this as well! If we can't answer a person's question, it

is all right to say, "That is a good question and I need to give it some more thought. Can we get together and talk later?" Admitting we don't know everything acknowledges their intelligence and provides an opportunity to continue a relationship.

6. *Care that is greater than conversion.* Not everyone will immediately convert. In fact, you may walk with people for years and see very little change. But can you continue showing love anyway? I remember a Muslim who observed, "Christians are always very friendly when we first meet. Then they try to convert me to Christianity. But when I don't, they begin to distance themselves. They don't want to be around me anymore." To her it seemed like Christians cared only as long as she was a potential convert. But remember, we are called to show love regardless. Jesus didn't start distancing Himself from Judas because He knew this wasn't going to be a successful project. The Bible says that Jesus loved His disciples "unto the end."[b]

7. *The message of the kingdom connects!* Most individuals in America carry some concept of Christianity. They may see it in a positive light, feel negative about it, or even feel injured and abused by it. Many angry callers just want to vent their frustration. They cannot understand why people insist on hanging on to what they consider an archaic way of seeing the world—blindly believing something that science has refuted. But regardless where they are coming from, there is a universal longing. When they hear that Jesus actually came to transform lives and bring a society where justice reigns and where people would rather suffer evil than inflict it, they are intrigued. For

---

[b] John 13:1

many, this is not the picture of Christianity they are familiar with. Our world is full of lonely people, and millions feel alienated. It can be life-changing to hear for the first time that God desires a world where the elderly and handicapped are cared for, where children don't suffer, and where every person, regardless of race, gender, or culture, can belong.

8. *It is essential that we see people through eyes of compassion.* The Apostle Paul told the church at Ephesus, "Therefore watch, and remember, that by the space of three years I ceased not to warn every one night and day with tears."[c] He had been warning them for years, but he had been doing this from the platform of tears. I have wondered how much different our evangelistic endeavors would turn out if more heartfelt tears were involved, if people could tell by my voice, my choice of words, and yes, by my tears, that I really care about them. Every encounter eventually ends. But when that person walks away or hangs up the phone, will he feel cared for? If we truly look at the lost through eyes of compassion, I think they will feel loved.

So where do we go, and what do we do with all this? It is great to learn how to interact with unbelievers, but how do we actually put all this into practice on a daily basis? The accounts we read of billboard calls are a little unique. The men answering these calls have the advantage of people calling them with questions, and most of us do not have that opportunity. So what can we do? We need to understand that if we are going to touch the lives of unbelievers and have meaningful conversations, we will need to spend time with them. I don't know where you are, but I encourage you to analyze your life. How could you develop relationships with neighbors, coworkers, or other acquaintances?

---

[c] Acts 20:31

There are two areas we need to examine closely if we are going to reach America with the Gospel. The first is our personal life. How much am I really willing to sacrifice to reach my neighbor? The second area is that of our own limitations. We will need to humbly admit we can't do everything, and God has given each of us different gifts. Let's start with our own personal life and passion.

Personal Passion

Recently I read about a man in Idaho who went to great lengths to pursue his passion for fishing. Stephen Veals committed to a project he called his 365 Challenge, in which he resolved to go fishing every single day in 2018. He had a full-time job and a family, so this required some creative scheduling. At the beginning of the year, Stephen laid out some ground rules for his 365 Challenge. He committed to fishing a minimum of fifteen minutes a day and doing it regardless of circumstances. It also had to be a body of water where there was a decent chance of catching fish. In other words, he had to get his line wet every day and it could not be in his children's swimming pool.

This commitment required tremendous sacrifice. There were times when he had to travel, and it wasn't easy to find a place to fish— or the time. But he was successful. He caught lots of fish (including a 6 ½-foot sturgeon), made lots of memories, and got his story in the newspaper. His reasons were simple: He wanted to do something he enjoyed, to reconnect with what was important in life, and to encourage others to escape the rat race and try it as well. "You can do a 365-day challenge with whatever makes you happiest," he told the reporter. "Try fifteen minutes a day for yourself. Day by day, you'll be surprised at how much you accomplish."[25]

As I read this, I marveled at this man's passion and commitment, but then I had to examine myself. Do I have that kind of commitment to using my home, my business, and my personal time to reach out to others? We can teach about evangelism, go to mission conferences, or listen to good messages on the topic. But if I am not actually spending time with unbelievers, I am not much different than the man who discusses the finer points of dieting while downing his second Big Mac with fries.

Accepting My Limitations

We can have a tendency to feel responsible for every lost soul out there, and many times this drives us to either employ wide-brush strategies in an attempt to save the masses, or subconsciously surrender and abandon the pursuit. The former is usually ineffective and can actually harm potential seekers. And when we give up and decide it's not worth the effort, we are ignoring the clear command of Scripture. Many times we then feel forced to develop unbiblical theology to defend this position.[d]

I'd like to encourage you to continue reaching out, while at the same time accepting your limitations. God is already at work in the lives of people around you. He is calling them to Himself, but He is asking you to join Him in this work. Most of us will never be called to win the masses, but we are called to touch the lives we come in contact with.

It is amazing how Jesus introduced His kingdom. He spent a few intense years focusing primarily on just twelve men. Further, it appears that He spent additional time concentrating on the personal development of just three of them—Peter, James, and John. If this was Jesus' strategy, why do we assume we should reach out in a different way? It is so easy to get involved in big programs. But what if each of us would commit to simply working intensively with a few seekers during the next year? What if every member of your local congregation would personally disciple one or two neighbors? As I have watched how individuals who seem to be effective and have a gift for evangelism operate,

---

[d] Various churches throughout history have concluded that the Great Commission has already been fulfilled. Others have decided that some churches are called to evangelism but others are not. Both of these beliefs are extremely weak theological positions.

I don't see them trying to do great things. Rather, I see them working with the people God has placed in their path. Sometimes it is only one or two. If all believers would simply dedicate their businesses, homes, and personal lives to God, I believe amazing things could happen!

Conclusion

The very first command given in the Bible is to "be fruitful and multiply,"[e] and it should be obvious to every lover of God or observer of creation that God loves multiplication. God wants to see expansion and growth, and the final words of Jesus to His disciples as He left this world was a command to go out and make disciples. God loves multiplication and increase! So how does God regard a church today that has lost His passion for expansion?

Consider for a moment a newly married couple who discovers they are unable to have children. They will go to multiple doctors, read articles on infertility, and stop at almost nothing to rectify the situation. Why? Because an inability to reproduce is not the norm. Something is wrong, and couples become alarmed when this does not happen. I would suggest this is also true in our churches. If our churches are not able to reproduce and plant more churches, we should be alarmed. In fact, we should be startled into action![26]

May the Lord bless you as you prayerfully analyze your personal life. Be willing to honestly evaluate your life from a Biblical perspective, and listen to the Spirit of God as He points out changes that need to be made. Be willing to reexamine your vision and purpose as a church. Go back often to those first believers in the book of Acts and examine their fervor and zeal for the kingdom. May the Lord bless and empower you and your local congregation as you demonstrate Jesus, right here in America.

---

[e] Genesis 1:28

Appendix:
Billboard Calls

Following is a selection of additional billboard calls. As in the earlier chapter of calls, the caller names are fictitious and the Phone Team Member answering the call is identified as the PTM.

1. Atheists and Agnostics:

Lucas

After driving past a sign boldly declaring "Jesus can free you from sin," Lucas called and began sharing his story. As a young man, he was a devout follower of Jesus. His church had a good pastor, and Lucas felt called to be an evangelist. But then his pastor died and was replaced by a man who became critical of Lucas.

Lucas: "I became discouraged and started going to bars. I met men in the bars on Saturday night who would go to church the next morning as Sunday school teachers. This hypocrisy got to me, and I finally got to the point I wanted nothing to do with God. I began to believe that Christianity was a farce, and I became an atheist."

Lucas described how his life had spiraled out of control and he ended up losing everything, including his wife and family. "Now I am divorced and remarried. I saw this billboard and it stirred something within me. Do you think anyone actually lives a life free from sin?"

PTM: "Believers may take a step in sin, but they can no longer walk in sin. At the new birth a seed was placed in them that fights against sin and keeps them from freely practicing sin again."

Lucas: "I have considered returning to Christ, but I am afraid I will go out on some limb and make a fool of myself again."

PTM: "I would encourage you to read and study the Gospels and let Jesus speak for Himself. It does make me sad to hear that you are divorced and remarried. You will find that Jesus commands against this."

Lucas: "I know. It makes me sad too."

Alex

Alex began by stating emphatically that he is not a Christian due to many unanswered questions. He has concerns about the early church and believes that the Council of Nicaea in 325 A.D. was a corrupt attempt to join church and state—an endeavor to create a Bible that would coerce people to come under church authority.

PTM: "But Alex, you need to understand that the New Testament canon was actually compiled at a later council, and when they did this they were actually confirming the writings that had already been accepted by the church earlier. One of the criteria for including a book in the canon was that it had to have been quoted by one of the early church fathers."

Alex: "Then why didn't they include all the gospel writings?"

PTM: "The spurious gospels you are referring to were actually written many years later. The Gospels that are in our New Testament, with the exception of John, were written before the destruction of Jerusalem in A.D. 70. Jesus prophesied the destruction of Jerusalem in the Gospels, but the event itself is not described. If they had been written after A.D. 70, the event would be described."

Alex had more questions about the accuracy of the Bible and how it was compiled. Then he wanted to know why there are miracles all through the Bible and yet we don't see any today.

PTM: "There are 40 recorded miracles in the Old Testament over a span of 4000 years. That's an average of one miracle per century. We then have many miracles surrounding Jesus to prove His claims, and we have miracles surrounding the apostles to establish their authority and to lay down the foundation for the church. We do see miracles today, but usually not on the scale of these miracles of the Bible. God doesn't waste miracles. He doesn't do miracles just to humor us. When a miracle is needed, God does it. I am satisfied to let God decide whether I see any miracles. I trust Him because of the evidence surrounding the Gospel and because of what He has done in my own life."

Alex: "Well, I will need to do more research before coming to a conclusion."

Oliver

Oliver began the conversation by stating up front that he is spiritual but not religious. Oliver's father was an MS-13 gang member, and his mother was impulsive and abusive. Consequently, his formative years were spent with his grandfather, who had broad religious beliefs, including reincarnation. Oliver shared several near-death experiences in which he believes he died and was brought back to life. This has caused him to give thought to the existence of a God.

> Oliver: "I am afraid to commit myself to any one faith or belief, for fear I will be wrong and be judged in the end. I have just tried to accept the good in all of them. This way none of them can condemn me in the end."

> PTM: "But Oliver, Jesus' claim is very exclusive. Jesus said, "I am the way, the truth, and the life: no man cometh unto the Father, but by me."[a] It isn't intellectually honest to say you believe in the words and teachings of Jesus and believe in other gods at the same time."

He went on to share with Oliver what following Jesus looks like, assuring him that the way of Jesus is a path of forgiveness, love, and nonviolence. These are virtues that will never harm anyone. This conversation took almost an hour, and Oliver was intrigued by the idea of Jesus introducing a kingdom, or an ideal society, that would enable people to live in harmony.

Blake

Blake said he has been passing these billboards many times and wondered what denomination of Christians we represent. After the team member told him we are Anabaptists, there was a lengthy discussion

---

[a] John 14:6

about discipleship, what it means to follow Jesus, and how the kingdom concept of Christianity differs from other perspectives. Blake then wanted to know what we believe about homosexuality, and when a Scripture reference was given he finally got to the issue that bothered him most—whether the Bible could be trusted.

> Blake: "So you just take the Bible and believe anything in it with blind faith?"
>
> PTM: "No, true faith isn't blind. That would be superstition. Our faith is based on evidence we have seen in lives, and in the many ways Biblical truth lines up with reality. For example, people in the past have reasoned that divorce and remarriage, in the case of unhappy homes, could result in a happier life for everyone, including the children. But the jury is in, and we now know that broken marriages result in a broken society. We now have evidence that we can trust the Bible even when experience has not yet shown the consequences for disobeying the message."
>
> Blake: "But what about homosexuality?"
>
> PTM: "The consequences for homosexuality are not yet completely evidenced, but you can be sure that experience will vindicate the Biblical position on this issue."
>
> Blake: "Very interesting! I have never heard anyone explain it like that."

The PTM went on to describe how the kingdom of God fulfills the longings in every heart. Communism has always ended in disaster because of selfishness. But the death and resurrection of Jesus provides the remedy for self-centeredness and makes the ideals we long for achievable. Blake wasn't completely convinced but had to admit that he has these same longings. In the past, he has always heard Christianity described as a formula to escape hell—that once a man believes, he can live as he wants but still go to heaven when he dies. This has always bothered him.

Jack

Jack freely admitted that he is skeptical of the Bible and identified himself as an agnostic. He could not understand how anyone could believe in the creation account when almost all the geologists and scientists agree that the earth is millions of years old. As they talked, Jack said he had been raised in a Christian home, and it would be much easier for him to still be a Christian. All of his family members are still believers, and he is the only one in his family who has rejected it. The PTM took him to the evidences for the resurrection of Jesus, and Jack conceded that evidence does exist. The discussion then turned to the teachings of Jesus, and what our world might look like if everyone loved their enemy, shared their wealth, and was faithful in their relationships. This seemed to open Jack's eyes to the beauty of the Gospel, and he readily agreed to receive several books that might help him on his journey. As the call ended, Jack concluded by saying, "Maybe my disagreement isn't with true Christianity, but rather with American Christianity!"

Reggie

This unbeliever began by immediately challenging the authenticity and origin of the Scriptures. He was friendly, but like many skeptics and scoffers today, Reggie had embraced a false understanding of how our Bible came into being.

> Reggie: "The Gospels were not even written down until a hundred years after the fact, and your Bible wasn't even compiled until hundreds of years later. How can those writings be accurate if they were written that long after the events took place?"
>
> PTM: "First of all, the Gospels were recorded much earlier. In fact, two of the Gospels were written by men who were Jesus' disciples during His ministry, and the other two were written

by men who were likely His followers as well. All of the New Testament except for the Revelation is believed to have been written before A.D. 70, within forty years of Jesus' crucifixion and resurrection. Secondly, when the canon of Scripture was officially approved, they were only ratifying what local churches had generally agreed upon for years. We have abundant evidence in the early Christian writings that the Scriptures we have are accurate."

At the conclusion of the call, Reggie was not totally convinced, but he had much to consider and seemed thankful for the information.

Arthur

> Arthur: "How much sin can I commit and still get to heaven? It's all about getting to heaven, isn't it?"
>
> PTM: "No, it isn't."

This response seemed to confuse him. Arthur had assumed, from what he had heard, that the primary goal of Christianity is to get a person to heaven after he dies. The PTM explained that Jesus came to initiate the kingdom of heaven here on earth, and God requires us to join that kingdom now if we want to be a part of it later. He also explained that the way of salvation provides entrance into the kingdom of heaven. Arthur liked this concept but decided he would rather wait till the end of his life before joining this kingdom.

> PTM: "You might be able to do this, but in the meantime you will be making selfish decisions that will make you a different person over time. You won't be the same person at the end of your life that you are now. Furthermore, you are presuming upon life and assuming you will have the opportunity to repent at the end of your life. And even if God does allow you to have enough time to repent, it isn't likely that you will want to do

so after a lifetime of hardening your heart."

Arthur: "Well, I understand what you are saying, but I will need to think about it a little more."

PTM: "I would encourage you to read the Gospels, especially Matthew 5, 6, and 7. Another passage you should consider is 1 Corinthians 6:9-11. These verses tell us things that will not be practiced in Christ's kingdom, and tell us that the power of Christ can help us change these behaviors."

After twenty minutes on the phone, Arthur was sobered, and Christianity was starting to appear differently than he had assumed.

Harry

People call the billboard number with different attitudes. Some are friendly and seriously searching for answers, while others simply vent their frustration. This one was a venter, and he refused to give his name, although we're calling him Harry. His first statement was a forceful, "God's not real!"

PTM: "Would you mind telling me what proof you have of that? And would you mind sharing your name?"

Harry: "I am not going to tell you anything about me."

PTM: "Well, I understand. When people are bound by sin, they live in fear and don't want to reveal anything about themselves. You see, I know exactly how that feels. There was a time in my life when I lived this way, but Jesus Christ has set me free."

The PTM then shared his first and last name with Harry. He also shared his own struggle to believe and told him what a blessing it has been to find salvation through Jesus. Harry kept trying to throw the conversation off course.

Harry: "So, will I go to hell because I am gay?"

PTM: "Well, the Bible says we shouldn't be deceived, that neither 'fornicators, nor idolaters, nor adulterers, nor effeminate, nor abusers of themselves with mankind, nor thieves, nor covetous, nor drunkards, nor revilers, nor extortioners, shall inherit the kingdom of God.'[b] In other words, all sin needs to be repented of if we want to be saved. But God has given us the opportunity to be born again through Jesus, and through the new birth we can be cleansed from our past sins."

At this point the PTM became aware that others were listening as well, so he spent some time describing the new birth and the importance of holiness in our lives. Finally Harry interrupted, saying he was going to go commit an act of immorality with his boyfriend. The PTM then decided to conclude the call and offered to pray for Harry.

Harry: "Please don't do that!"

PTM: "Okay, I will just pray for you after we conclude our conversation."

Harry: "Please do not!"

PTM: "Well, my desire is that you can find deliverance through Jesus."

Harry: "I hope you go to hell!"

After concluding the call, the PTM prayed for him. Harry's adversarial tone had continued throughout this difficult eleven-minute conversation. It has been said that the message of the Gospel will make one glad, sad, or mad. In this case, it seemed to make him mad.

Charlie and Oscar

Charlie said he was a Christian, while his friend Oscar professed to be

---

[b] 1 Corinthians 6:9, 10

an atheist. They had been traveling along arguing about the origin of life when they saw a sign proclaiming "There IS Evidence for GOD." So they decided to call. Charlie spoke first, saying he had only been a Christian for several years. He had been trying to explain to his atheist friend Oscar what the Bible says about creation, but he did not feel like he was doing a good job of it. Oscar then told a little of his background. He had been raised Mormon, but had turned away from religion after being abused by a Mormon bishop.

After listening to both of them, the PTM spent time sharing facts that point to a Creator. He talked about the complexity of the universe and the absurdity of declaring that nothing can create something. The only logical conclusion, when observing the complexity of nature, is that it must have come from a very intelligent, all-powerful God. A human chromosome contains one hundred million Encyclopedia Britannica pages worth of information. Saying that all this came together by chance is preposterous. The chances of a protein coming together by random chance has similar odds to millions of blind men simultaneously solving a Rubik's cube. The odds of this occurring are simply too unbelievable and ludicrous for a rational human to accept. Whenever you see a building, you know there must be a builder. Consequently, the intricacy of creation demands a Creator. This is powerful evidence for an all-powerful God.

Ryan

This call began with Ryan saying he had never heard of Jesus. He said he wants to know how to get to heaven, but he doesn't know anything about Jesus. The PTM sensed that something was wrong and finally told Ryan he was not sure he was being completely honest. Ryan then confessed that he actually goes to church every Sunday but doesn't agree with what is being taught. He is 35 years old, an atheist, and yet afraid to tell his parents and friends that he no longer believes.

The PTM tried to explain the basis of our faith, the evidences for a Creator, and pointed to the many observable facts that indicate an ultimate designer. All evidence points to the fact that space, time, and matter needed to have a beginning, so whatever created these must be outside of and greater than space, time, and matter. Obviously, something immaterial and timeless would be God.

Many times during the discussion, Ryan would agree with the logic, but he finally asked the question that had been bothering him. "So how can there be thousands of different types of Christianity, and yet you believe that your type is the correct one? How can you be sure your brand of Christianity will be correct in the end?"

> PTM: "Well, understand, Ryan, it isn't my brand of Christianity that will be correct. It will be the type that agrees with what God has revealed in Scripture. Let's start with the church you attend. You said earlier that you believe your church is doing very well, and that the people who attend are living good lives. So what does the military call their opponent?"
>
> Ryan: "The enemy?"
>
> PTM: "That is correct. And what does Jesus say we should do to our enemies?"
>
> Ryan: "We should love them."
>
> PTM: "So, does your church support war and killing the enemy?"
>
> Ryan: "Yes, they do support our military."
>
> PTM: "Okay, but that goes directly against what Jesus taught. The Bible also says that women should cover their heads when they pray or prophesy. Do your women do this?"
>
> Ryan: "No, they don't."
>
> PTM: "The Bible also says that women should adorn themselves in modest apparel with shame-facedness and sobriety. Do

your women dress modestly?"

Ryan: "No, they don't always."

PTM: "So, Ryan, can you really say that your church is following the teachings of Jesus? Maybe you need to study your Bible and start asking some questions."

Ryan: "Okay, and thanks for this conversation!"

PTM: "And I suspect, Ryan, that as you begin to study the Bible and see the truth in God's Word, you will become converted yourself."

Ryan: "Wow, that would be a miracle! That definitely could happen!"

At the end of the hour-long call, Ryan seemed willing to take up the challenge. He agreed to study the Bible for himself and to try to learn what authentic Christianity really looks like.

Nathan

The tone in Nathan's voice was carefree, and he began by casually asking, "Howdy, am I going to heaven or to hell?"

PTM: "Well, it is only the followers of Jesus who are going to the place where Jesus dwells."

Nathan: "I think it's cool to follow Jesus, but my mother taught me to just be myself. If other people want to be controlled by someone else, that's all right. But I want to be my own boss!"

PTM: "The book of Proverbs in the Bible says, 'There is a way which seemeth right unto a man, but the end thereof are the ways of death.'[c] The prophet Jeremiah wrote, 'It is not in man

---

[c] Proverbs 14:12

that walketh to direct his steps.[d] This means that we don't have enough wisdom ourselves to always make good choices. Being our own boss means we will make decisions we later regret. But Jesus leads us to make choices we will never regret."

Nathan: "Well, I am going to drink, smoke pot, and enjoy my sex life and die before I have any regrets."

PTM: "Remember, death does not end our existence. Those who refuse to follow Jesus will ultimately be separated from Him—the one who is the source of everything that is good and perfect!"

Nathan: "I just want to be free!"

PTM: "Jesus said it is truth that actually sets a man free. He told us if we will continue in His Word, we will be His disciples. We will know the truth and will be free indeed![e] Today there are men lying on the sidewalks in the slums of New York. These men wanted to be free and to do their own thing. But today they are abandoned and destitute."

Nathan: "I don't care about all that! I just want to have my own way and do my own thing!"

Riley

Riley: "I am not religious, but was wondering why you go to the bother and expense of putting up all these billboards."

PTM: "Let's start by focusing on the word 'truth' in our phone number. Those of us who study God's Word believe that truth corresponds to reality. Jesus said He is the truth, and we believe to live in reality we need to follow Jesus."

---

[d] Jeremiah 10:23

[e] John 8:31, 32

Riley: "But I noticed on the billboard you have the evolution symbol crossed out. Ninety percent of scientists believe in evolution. Why would you go against logic?"

PTM: "Science and logic are built upon empirical evidence. We see no evidence that information can arrange itself. Empirical observation tells us that when we see arranged information it was organized by an intelligent being. And we find inexhaustible information in the tens of thousands of DNA codes, all of which are incomprehensibly complicated. To believe that these sophisticated arrangements all happened by chance is to fly in the face of scientific observation."

Riley: "Don't you think we should just have the humility to say we don't know?"

PTM: "But we do know. The evidence overwhelmingly points to a supernatural intelligence. To say 'I don't know' in such a case is not humility."

Riley understood the logic but wasn't quite ready to agree. The PTM encouraged Riley to read the Gospels and let Jesus speak for Himself. He explained the way of repentance, of surrender to the King, of obedient discipleship, and concluded by noting that our ideals cannot be realized until our selfishness is conquered through Jesus.

George

George was a bitter man. There was a time when things were different. He said he had once been a Christian and had even served on the mission field for a number of years. But today he is upset and no longer sure that God even exists. George's 26-year-old daughter has been suffering from Crohn's disease for the past twenty years. He quoted Scriptures, like Mark 16:18, where Jesus said that His disciples will lay their hands on the sick and they will recover. He has prayed for his daughter repeatedly, but she has not been healed.

He was extremely upset, raising his voice at times, not at the PTM personally, but out of bitterness and frustration that he had trusted the Bible, but it had let him down. The PTM listened for some time and then shared out of his own experience. He also has a daughter who has been sick for a number of years, and he took George to 1 John. "Here John addresses another aspect to answered prayer. 'And this is the confidence that we have in him, that, if we ask any thing according to his will, he heareth us: and if we know that he hear us, whatsoever we ask, we know that we have the petitions that we desired of him.'[f] We know that God hears us, but God is only going to grant our petition if it is according to His will. We don't always understand everything God is trying to accomplish in our lives and in the world, so we must trust that God knows best. It is also important to seek the balance of Scriptures on these issues."

> PTM: "George, I know Jesus is real. He saved me and changed my life. So I'm not going to walk away from Jesus just because I don't understand everything He is doing."

> George: "Well, that's not where I am, and I guess you could consider me an atheist now. If there is a God, He didn't even answer my prayer to heal my daughter in spite of all those years that I served the Lord in ministry."

As the PTM tried to encourage him, George continued to spew out his bitterness, his sentences interspersed with curse words. His daughter's medical situation had definitely shaken his faith in God. "Why not believe in other religions?" he shouted. "Why only Christianity?" The PTM took him back to the resurrection, a validation of who Jesus is. It is an account George knew well, but it seemed the fact that God was not answering his prayer to heal his daughter was too much.

---

[f] 1 John 5:14, 15

In the end George did thank the PTM for listening and caring. After hanging up, the PTM was very concerned about him. He sent George a text saying, "Please don't do anything to hurt yourself. Remember, your family needs you, and I am praying for you!"

2. Struggling or Facing a Crisis

James

Raised Roman Catholic, James said he became disillusioned with faith. He left religion and now calls himself science-oriented, concluding that all of life's questions can be answered without religion. But after leaving his church, James had an experience with mind-altering drugs that convinced him there is something beyond the tangible. He is now willing to concede that there is a higher power behind life and the natural order, but he believes evolution was the process by which the world as we know it came to be.

> PTM: "But James, we don't see evidence in nature of species changing or life improving over time through evolution. For example, scientists have generated millions of generations of fruit flies, but they are still fruit flies. And the mutated ones are deformed, not bettered by the mutations."

> James: "I know, and I have wondered about that as well. But it's not just creation, there is something else that bothers me about religion. Why do we need a standard outside of man himself? Many marriages are just incompatible. Why force people to stay married to someone they are not compatible with?"

> PTM: "Many couples today fornicate before marriage, so the process of evaluating and comparing their goals, temperaments, and beliefs is short-circuited. God commanded that the physical relationship is to be delayed until marriage, giving a couple the

ability to focus on their compatibility before they are married."

James said he understood, though he went on to reveal that he is living with his girlfriend in the dorm of the college where he is pursuing a biology major. James was unusually transparent about his confusion and was willing to acknowledge the truths the PTM presented. At the end of the call he said, "I am so glad I saw the billboard. All my life I have been asking questions and couldn't find answers. You have been helpful." The PTM encouraged James to study the Gospels and learn more about Jesus. James said he didn't have a Bible, so one was sent to him.

Natalie

Seeing a billboard that said "After you die, you will meet God," Natalie decided to call and inquire. "What happens after we die?"

> PTM: "Well, before I answer that, let me ask you a question. Do you believe in the Scriptures? Do you believe the Bible is truth?"

> Natalie: "Well, I grew up going to church, but now I'm not sure."

> PTM: "Thank you for your honesty. The reality is that every one of us has to decide on our own if the Bible is true or not. At a deep level, all of us want truth."

> Natalie: "You are right, and I really want to know what is right!"

> PTM: "So let me explain how I have come to believe that the Bible is true. There are several reasons, but one of them is the Bible's transparent origins. There is nothing secretive about how the Jewish Ten Commandments or the rest of their law came into being. The Bible is very clear that God gave His law to Israel in a very public way. Many thousands of people saw the marvelous way that God worked with Israel. The same is true after Jesus was resurrected. The Bible says that on the day of Pentecost the Spirit of God came down and worked in a

miraculous way. And it was done very publicly."

Natalie: "But why would that matter?"

PTM: "Because these accounts were written down and distributed while the people who had observed it were still alive. If the written record wasn't correct, there were people who could have spoken up. However, they didn't. We don't have any record of someone saying, 'Hey, I was there, and this isn't what happened.' Do you understand?"

Natalie: "I'm following you."

PTM: "Now, contrast this to other religions. Buddhism, Mormonism, Islam—all of these religions were founded by an individual who went off in the woods somewhere, got a revelation from God, came back out and said, 'I have no proof of this, but this is what God told me. I want you to believe and trust me because I am a good fellow.' "

Natalie: "I'd never thought about that."

PTM: "Beyond this, the Bible has been proven archaeologically, scientifically, and historically. These are some of the reasons I trust the Bible. When we accept the Bible as truth, we see what the Bible says about repentance, a change of heart, a change of mind, and a change of allegiance. And we observe the impact following its truths has on our own life, as well as the lives of others, our confidence continues to grow."

Savannah

After the initial greeting, Savannah started in with some challenging questions.

Savannah: "I have drifted spiritually and have some questions. One thing I can't understand is why the Bible has teachings in it that are unfair to women. For example, it teaches that a raped woman is required to marry the man who raped her! How is that fair? That just condones rape!"

PTM: "We need to understand the context in which some of these laws were given. In the Old Testament, God was bringing people out of a viciously wicked culture where women and slaves had no rights and were being abused. But a careful reading of all these laws shows that God was not condoning abuse. In fact, the laws He gave actually served to limit it. Even at that time God was looking ahead to a new kingdom where His people would not do such evils. That is why He sent His Son Jesus."

Savannah: "But I thought Jesus came so people could be forgiven, so when they die they won't go to hell."

PTM: "Jesus did die so we can be forgiven, but He also came to do much more. Jesus came to introduce a kingdom where people would be governed by the Spirit of God living within them. This kingdom is what God has always had in mind. The church today is to be loving the hurting, caring for the handicapped, and sharing their wealth with those who lack. This is what Jesus taught! Unfortunately, many have forgotten the kingdom that Jesus taught and just focus on getting to heaven after they die."

Following this dialogue, there was a lengthy discussion about evolution, morality, and parts of the Bible that she believes have been corrupted. Savannah said she is bisexual and thinks some of the passages dealing with sexuality have been mistranslated. She was obviously acquainted with the Bible.

The PTM took her to Romans 1, read verses 26 and 27, and then explained that homosexuality violates the kingdom ideal that God has in mind. "The Bible is not a textbook of ideas to be manipulated, but a revelation of Jesus Christ. The honest person finds there a clear picture of Jesus, a clear statement of His teachings, and clear instructions about how Jesus can salvage his life."

Toward the end, Savannah admitted that she really didn't believe in the God of the Bible but considers herself a pantheist, believing that God is in and a part of everything. In other words, God and the universe are the same.

> PTM: "Let me share my thoughts on pantheism. This belief has some fundamental problems and isn't consistent with what we observe in science and the natural world. The maker of something never becomes part of the thing that he made. He exists outside of it, and we see this in the God of the Bible. He existed before the universe and is greater than the universe He created."

The conversation ended on a congenial note, with Savannah thanking the PTM for talking with her.

Logan

Logan is attending college, and the sinful party life on campus has a grip on him. He knows that his participation in alcohol, drugs, and sex is destroying him and prays to God each night for forgiveness. But he can't seem to stop. The PTM asked if there is a Christian fellowship on campus that might be of help to him.

> Logan: "Oh yes, I go to the Christian fellowship meetings. I also have a good church and Christian parents behind me, and I have some good Christian friends. In short, I have all the accountability I need, and I know that the pleasures are temporary in contrast to the true satisfaction of a long-range approach, but I just can't stop."

> PTM: "Well, Logan, the Bible says to 'keep thy heart with all

diligence; for out of it are the issues of life.'[8] The decisions you are making each day are actually making you who you are. Earlier you said that when you leave college you hope to leave all this sin behind you and marry a fine Christian lady. But you are deceiving yourself! You are assuming you will have the same pure aspirations when you leave college that you do now. If you think you cannot break free now, it will be even harder after several years of growing your sinful habits."

After giving Logan additional strong warnings, the PTM prayed with him and offered to contact him in a week or two to provide additional accountability.

Lydia

Lydia had seen a number of billboards in the large city where she lives. She had just seen one asking "Where are you going, heaven or hell?" and desperately wanted help. She was 49 years old, had been on drugs for many years, and cried as she tried to talk. She has had many live-in partners, only one of whom she has been married to, and now lives with a man who has three children. By her own admission, her life is a mess. But the issue that bothers her the most is that she had an abortion. She cried pitifully while trying to explain how this sin bothers her, summarizing by saying, "It eats on my soul every day!"

The PTM encouraged Lydia to cry out to Jesus, but she doesn't believe she can be forgiven. She continued to share more sins she has been involved in. One of these was involvement with an Ouija board and the evil that had come from this encounter. Many of her friends have overdosed and died, and she doesn't have anyone she can turn to. Recently Lydia had a near-death experience when an aneurysm burst in her brain. Everyone thought she was going to die, but she

---

[8] Proverbs 4:23

miraculously recovered. She wondered if perhaps God was giving her another chance.

> PTM: "Lydia, God is giving you another opportunity. I would like you to take your Bible, turn to the book of Matthew, and start reading. As you do this, pray to God and ask Him to reveal Jesus Christ to you. Your sin right now looks like a huge mountain that is so high you can never get over it. But what you need is Jesus Christ to lead you over this mountain. As you read through Matthew, keep a notebook handy and write down any verse that you don't understand. Then after you have some questions, you can call back, and I will discuss these passages with you."

> Lydia: "I would just like to be at peace. I look in the mirror, and all I see is ugliness. I am such a false person, but I will try."

Matthew

Matthew belongs to an Anabaptist group and called because he is depressed most of the time.

> PTM: "So, specifically, what are you depressed about?"

> Matthew: "It isn't anything specific. I try to do what is right, but I fail, and then I feel so defeated."

> PTM: "This condemnation you are feeling is from Satan. If it originated with the Holy Spirit, you would know what to do and would have peace in obeying the direction of the Holy Spirit. The devil's condemnations are always vague and filled with despair. You need to learn to distinguish between the voice of the Holy Spirit and the voice of the devil. Then you need to resist the devil by claiming the promises contained in the eighth chapter of Romans. Those who walk in the Spirit and in the light are never condemned by God, even if they fail, because

Christ's blood continually cleanses the person who is walking in the light."[h]

Matthew: "I have experienced the joy that comes from obedience. I was in town the other day with money to buy a new battery for my phone. I met a man who needed financial help, and I gave him half of my money. I found myself filled with such joy!"

PTM: "Yes, forgetting self and helping others is always a good way to help dispel depression."

Stella

Stella had been married for 23 years and has four children. For years, she was involved in sin over the internet, and a couple years ago she became convicted that this was wrong. She confessed her sin to her husband, but he refused to forgive her and is in the process of filing for divorce. Stella's husband took their children away from her and placed them in a boarding school. She has been living alone, and the divorce is to be finalized next month. All of this is overwhelming to her, although she realizes she is suffering the consequences of her own sin. For the last couple of years she has been praying for healing and asking God to restore her marriage and children, but nothing seems to be changing.

The PTM tried to encourage her. He told her if she has sincerely repented and put her faith in Christ, she is forgiven before God. Oftentimes we experience earthly consequences for our actions even though we have been exonerated by God. Stella feels like she never bonded with her mother, and now she is burdened by the reality that she has never bonded emotionally with her own children. The PTM encouraged her to keep praying, to read and memorize Scripture, and to try to find a mature Christian lady for support. Stella seemed to feel

---

[h] 1 John 1:7

better after sharing her burdens, and they prayed together before concluding the call.

Leon

Leon called saying he is experiencing a mid-life crisis, and everything seemed to be going wrong. "Every man has certain goals, but we seem to be living in a system that wants us to fail!" He is currently living in his car because the apartment where he was living burned down. He is waiting for a financial settlement before he seeks for another place to live. Leon has a job, but lacks a church. He said his last experience with a church was a great disappointment. "I went there to hear the Gospel, but they pressured us to keep giving more and more. They would pass the offering plate several times during the service. I got tired of that and just gave up. I believe in Jesus, but I don't believe in church."

> PTM: "God intends that we live in fellowship with other believers who can encourage, support, and pray for us. He wants the church to be a society of redeemed people who demonstrate heaven on earth, just like we pray in the Lord's Prayer."

> Leon: "But my marriage didn't turn out good either. We had a pure courtship and yet things eventually fell apart."

> PTM: "It sounds like you have been through some painful situations and have had a bad experience with a self-centered church. But don't give up! Look for a church that is attempting to live out the teachings of Jesus."

The PTM went on to describe what a New Testament church should look like. Leon seemed encouraged, saying, "You have helped me see what I need to do."

David

There are many billboards in the area where David lives. He has seen them for some time but never had any interest in calling until recently.

David had just been told that he has an incurable disease that will eventually take his life. He grew up around Christians and had several Bibles, but he never saw a need for religion or was even sure God existed. But his recent diagnosis had discouraged him, and he wasn't sure what to think about life and dying.

The PTM spoke to David of the importance of reading his Bible and learning to know God. Death is coming to all of us, and learning that we have an incurable disease can be a blessing in that it provides an opportunity to prepare for death. Impending death can be a merciful warning from God.

David said he ponders death more than he used to, but he is not sure what to think about it. Overall, he just feels discouraged and doesn't know what to do.

Lewis

"I am dying soon," was how Lewis succinctly described his concern. Only 19 years old, he had been diagnosed with cancer, and the doctors had given him less than a year to live. This news had shaken Lewis and he seemed stunned and bewildered. "I didn't grow up in a religious home. I guess my little sister went to Sunday school some, so she might be a Christian, but we were not religious and I don't know much about the Bible. I don't want to die! But I need to know more about God and how to get right with Him if I am going to die!"

The PTM talked with Lewis for some time, explaining what the Bible says about our sin, our broken relationship with our Creator, and the opportunity through Jesus that we have to be reconciled to God. The PTM offered to send a Bible, and Lewis was interested.

Lewis: "How big a book is the Bible?"

PTM: "The Bible is comprised of 66 separate books, or sections, but I wouldn't recommend that you try reading all of them immediately. I suggest you start in the book of Matthew and discover who Jesus is. As you continue reading, you will find out how to commit to Jesus and have a relationship with Him."

Lewis: "But what about my physical healing? Will God heal me?"

PTM: "God may choose to heal you. But He is primarily interested in healing you spiritually. He can very easily take away your cancer if He chooses to. God knows what is best for you and you will need to leave that up to Him. The first thing you must do is get right with God by repenting of your sins and committing your life to Jesus Christ. If you are willing, I will send you a Bible and we can talk more later."

Lewis: "Yes, please send me a Bible."

Tom

Tom saw a billboard while walking through town and called because he is worried about COVID-19. He and his wife live in an area hit hard by the coronavirus and is concerned that their family will contract the virus. They have a small son who likes to touch things, so good sanitation is difficult.

Tom: "As I watch what is happening in New York City, sometimes I feel overwhelmed. I don't know whether or not there is a God, so I just call myself a skeptic. But there is something inside me that says there has to be a plan for how things are in our universe."

PTM: "So, Tom, why do you think you have feelings like this? How do you believe our world came into being?"

Tom: "I don't know, but this coronavirus thing has made me ponder these questions."

3. Creation versus Evolution

Dexter

Dexter and his three friends saw a billboard proclaiming "In the beginning God created," and he was curious. Why would someone pay to put up a billboard proclaiming an ancient belief that had been debunked years ago? After telling the PTM that he was on speakerphone, Dexter got to the point. "Evolution obviously has more evidence than creationism. So why would you still believe in creation by God?"

> PTM: "There are multiple reasons I believe in a Creator, and one of those is the evidence provided by DNA. Observation leads us to the conclusion that information never arranges itself, but rather requires an intelligent organizer. The belief that matter somehow arranged itself into countless inexhaustible codes with the ability to replicate themselves is not based on scientific observation but on incredible imagination."

> Dexter: "So if everything needs to be created, and you are saying that God created everything we see, then who made God?"

> PTM: "Good question. Logic leads us to an uncaused first cause. Something had to be first. Either God has always been and is eternal, or matter is. But if we decide that matter is eternal and created itself, then matter is an eternal creator. So we are back to the same place."

Dexter and his friends finally conceded that this was true but said this doesn't mean Christianity is the correct religion. So the PTM shared some of the evidences for the resurrection and urged all three men to read the Gospel of Luke and allow Jesus to speak for Himself.

Henry

His initial question was whether or not we believe in evolution. The PTM began by addressing the complexity of DNA and the need for an intelligent Creator, concluding by saying, "We believe God created everything directly." Henry had seen a sign stating "In the beginning God created," but he wasn't sure if we believed that evolution was the process God used.

> Henry: "I am a Roman Catholic, and my leaders teach us that much of the Bible is metaphorical, so some of what we read about creation in the Bible isn't intended to be taken literally."

> PTM: "I understand, but we need to be careful with this. Once we depart from a literal understanding of Scripture, it isn't long until the entire message becomes subjective and up for grabs."

> Henry: "But what do you do with all the scientific evidence? For example, there is a lot of radiometric evidence for an old earth rather than a young earth as suggested by the Bible. How do you reconcile this?"

> PTM: "I don't have much confidence in the accuracy of the radiometric testing used by geologists today, and even scientists who do not believe in the God of the Bible admit that there is a lot of guesswork involved."

> Henry: "But what about the hominids[i] that preceded humans?"

> PTM: "I have lived long enough to see scientists discover some supposed subhuman remains, only to conclude with more study that the specimen was fully human after all. This has occurred repeatedly, and I believe it will continue to happen as research continues."

After more discussion regarding origins and evolution, Henry asked why the PTM isn't a Roman Catholic. The PTM described the

---

[i] A classification used by evolutionists that includes great apes of the past which are now extinct, as well as humans, chimpanzees, gorillas, and orangutans.

Anabaptist movement, which objected to the union of church and state. He also shared the fact that true Christians repent and follow Jesus rather than focus on a "save-me, ticket-to-heaven" gospel promoted by many Protestant groups, or the penance system which allows people to disobey the clear teachings of Jesus. "I believe in the same Gospel the early Christians did," he told Henry. "They believed a true Christian is one who repents and then attempts to follow Jesus by the power of the Holy Spirit. I believe churches grieve God if they allow people to assume they are going to heaven while disobeying almost everything Jesus says."

Edward

Edward wanted evidence for God, so the PTM took him to the complexity in DNA and the obvious need for a designer. But Edward wasn't convinced and tried to insist that adaptations of species prove evolution. The conversation was very congenial, but he continued to insist that highly organized information alone is not evidence. He felt that if given enough time, evolution could form itself.

So the PTM took him back to origins. "Adaptation rearranges the genetic information, but where did the highly organized information come from in the first place? By life around us, we know that highly organized information is always the work of an intelligent being. Mutations and natural selection do not create information, Edward, but work with information that already exists."

Edward then tried to argue that life originated from a very simple cell, and the PTM attempted to show that this argument is outdated in light of new scientific proof. "Darwin believed that the single-celled organism was simple, but modern science has debunked that theory. The simplest single-celled amoeba is a more highly organized factory than anything designed by men. And further, all of it had to be in place at one time for life to even exist! There is no way it could have formed little by little."

Edward agreed that the odds that even a single-celled amoeba could evolve are extremely remote. He also understood that it is absurd to imagine that highly organized information could occur on its own. However, he kept insisting that evolution is more logical than creation. Edward was a very respectful conversationalist, and eventually they had to agree to disagree. Before finishing the call, the PTM encouraged Edward to study the Gospels. "You may find that Jesus represents a more compelling reality that you realize!"

Rory

Rory is a military veteran and wanted to hear the proof for a Creator. After a discussion about radiometric dating, the complexity of DNA, and whether or not an intelligent arranger was needed, Rory began to speak of the blessing that science has been to humanity.

> Rory: "Advances in science in the past few hundred years have been tremendous. I believe this points to the reality that things are getting better and our world is improving."

> PTM: "But Rory, these scientific advances have also made it possible for widespread human abuse and destruction. Because of new inventions, humanity can inflict much greater harm on others."

> Rory: "That is true. While humans have been very intelligent in their technological discoveries, they have also been very juvenile in their behavior. But I believe evolving human experience gives us a developing sense of what humans should do, and there is hope that sometime in the future humans will start treating each other better."

> PTM: "Historians say the twentieth century was the bloodiest in history. Would you say the happenings of the last century provide a basis for your hope?"

Rory: "No, you're correct. The last century was the worst in history, despite our scientific advancements."

PTM: "Many atheists agree that the teachings of Jesus, if actually practiced, would be the best hope for the world. Of course, atheists don't believe in the deity of Christ, but they admit that Jesus gave us the best ethic ever uttered. Would you agree?"

Rory: "Yes, I would. I believe Jesus was one of the greatest teachers who ever lived."

PTM: "But if we are going to credit Jesus as the greatest teacher ever, then we must take seriously what He said about Himself. Speaking of Himself, Jesus said, 'The Father loveth the Son, and hath given all things into his hand. He that believeth on the Son hath everlasting life: and he that believeth not the Son shall not see life; but the wrath of God abideth on him.'[j] Now those are strong words, and not something just any good teacher would say! Either Jesus was who He said He was, or He was mentally unstable and we shouldn't trust anything He said!"

Rory: "If Jesus was who He said He was, then why isn't His Gospel believed by most intelligent people? If Jesus was actually God, and the Bible obviously right, then the schools would be teaching this as fact."

PTM: "Because all of us, myself included, have an overwhelming desire to do as we please. And we have amazing capacities to rationalize our behavior to make what we want to do seem right even if it is patently wrong. We need a moral standard—a power and accountability outside of ourselves—to enable us to rise above our selfishness. Jesus came to help us overcome this self problem!"

---

[j] John 3:35, 36

Rory wasn't convinced of the need for a Creator at the end of the call, but he seemed genuinely intrigued by the kingdom ideals and agreed to get a Bible and study the Gospels.

> PTM: "As you read, ask yourself. 'What would happen if everyone believed Jesus actually meant every word He said? What would a world look like where everyone obeyed Jesus as King?' "

> Rory: "Wow, thanks for the good discussion! While we may not agree, I really enjoyed this. In fact, on a scale of 0 to 10, I rate this conversation a 9.5. I encourage you to keep the faith you have described, just as I intend to keep the faith I have described."

Max

Max wanted to know why our billboard has the evolution symbol crossed out. He seemed to be serious about being a Christian but believed in theistic evolution. After discussing various aspects of the debate between a young and old earth, the PTM told him: "The evolution of man poses a real problem."

> Max: "What do you mean?"

> PTM: "Well, if evolution is true, just when did God breathe into this evolutionary process to make man a living soul?"

> Max: "Yeah, that is a problem."

> PTM: "In addition, Max, theistic evolution requires lots of death taking place before man came into being. Yet the Bible says death came by sin.[k] So is it possible for millions of deaths to be occurring before man had even arrived and sinned?"

In the end Max agreed that God could very well have created everything immediately just as it says in a literal reading of Genesis 1.

---

[k] Romans 5:12

Throughout the dialogue, Max remained respectful and open, and the PTM encouraged him to keep seeking truth and not let this subject distract him from a focus on Jesus and full obedience to His teachings.

Louie

The sign had declared that there is evidence for God, so Louie called and said he would like someone to provide some proof. Louie said he was very interested in truth and honestly wanted to know why people believe there is a God.

> PTM: "So, Louie, if you walked down to a pond, and saw on the surface that the scum had been arranged into the Gettysburg Address, wouldn't you ask, 'Who did it?' You would intuitively know that the scum could not have arranged itself into an intelligent message, right?"
>
> Louie: "Of course, someone would have had to do it."
>
> PTM: "Absolutely. You would know that some intelligent being had to have been involved. Yet the DNA codes behind every living thing are inexhaustibly more complicated than that. This points to the fact that there must be an incredibly intelligent being out there."
>
> Louie: "Good point, and that is strong evidence for some kind of designer out there. But if you keep going with the numbers in pi, you will eventually see your phone number. Doesn't that show that chance can eventually create ordered information?"
>
> PTM: "But remember, a phone number is 10 digits at the most. DNA is incredibly more complex. Sir Fred Hoyle, a leading mathematician of the last century, said that the chance of obtaining the required set of enzymes for even the simplest living cell by chance was one followed by 40,000 zeroes. Since the number of atoms in the known universe is infinitesimally tiny

by comparison, even a whole universe full of primordial soup wouldn't have a chance. Real faith is based on evidence. But believing that our universe evolved by chance is superstition. God is not expecting us to believe in Him through blind faith. He has provided strong evidence of His existence in creation."

4. From Curious to Serious

Jamie

Educated in a Roman Catholic high school and now studying bio-physics at a Catholic university, Jamie said he isn't a Christian because he disagrees with some of the Biblical concepts he was taught. He especially struggles to believe that a loving God would create a situation in which anybody would experience the never-ending torture of hell.

PTM: "You might consider what C. S. Lewis said about hell. He said he believes that the gates of hell are barred from the inside. That is, those in hell are in rebellion against God. They would rather suffer in hell than submit to God."

Jamie: "But the whole thing about living in heaven forever seems so boring!"

PTM: "I would encourage you to consider the parable of the talents.[1] To the men who had used their talents well, the ruler said he would make them ruler over many things. These parables give the impression that we will be busy exercising the full use of our talents without any limitations in eternity. It doesn't sound like a boring existence to me! I would encourage you to set aside your current presuppositions about Jesus, read the Gospels again, and reconsider what God might actually have in mind."

---

[1] Matthew 25:14-30

Luke and Jessica

Luke and Jessica are college students. Seeing a billboard asking where you are going after you die, they decided to call. They were also intrigued by the phone number, which incorporated the word *truth*. Jessica was the primary spokesperson during the call, but Luke occasionally chimed in.

> Jessica: "I think this service you are providing seems pretty interesting, especially promoting the thought that you have truth. How do you know truth is with God?"
>
> PTM: "Excellent question. First, let's define what we mean by truth. Truth is reality, or the way things really are. Truth isn't just a philosophy. Truth must be that which actually exists. Do you believe truth does exist?"

Jessica hesitated a little before responding. She seemed to fear this discussion was going a little deeper than she had anticipated. But she eventually agreed that reality, and therefore truth, do exist. The PTM then spoke of his own life, of his struggle with belief, his investigation into the dependability of the Bible, and of his eventual conversion to Christianity. One of the things that greatly impacted him was coming to the realization that Jesus actually loved him enough to suffer and die. They listened respectfully, but Jessica didn't like the fact that the PTM had been persuaded to consider Christianity through something intangible like love. She felt we should limit truth to what science can prove and not use elusive aspects like feelings.

> PTM: "Jessica, is Luke your brother or a family member?"
>
> Jessica: "He's my boyfriend."
>
> PTM: "How do you feel about Luke? And how does he feel about you?"
>
> Jessica: "I love him, and he loves me."

PTM: "But Jessica, how do you know Luke loves you?"

Jessica: "Probably by how he responds to me and by his thoughtfulness."

PTM: "So it feels like he loves you. Would you say that the statement you made about Luke's love for you was actually truth? It sounds like it is just based on feelings. The reality is that truth does exist beyond the physical, naturalistic world. We learn much from science, but there are things we can know without scientific evidence."

Reuben

A friend had given him the phone number, and Reuben called with questions about heaven and hell. The PTM began by sharing about the relationship that God wants to have with us and taking Reuben to the words of Jesus just before He died. "And this is life eternal, that they might know thee the only true God, and Jesus Christ, whom thou hast sent."[m] The PTM then continued, "God wants to have a relationship with us, and He has a redemption plan that makes all things new!"

Reuben was a hungry soul who drank in the teaching about God. He has struggled with the existence of God. Years ago in school he saw a child being picked on and abused by other classmates. Even though he was very young, Reuben knew this was not right. He didn't understand how a God could be all-powerful and still allow this to occur. That was years ago, but Reuben still struggles with the pain and suffering in the world. If there is a God, how can He allow this to continue?

The PTM addressed the issue of suffering and pain, and why it came into the world. He explained that this was not God's original design, but is a result of man's choices. But a day is coming when every wrong will be made right.

---

[m] John 17:3

Reuben: "So, assuming there is a god, how do we know which one is really God? There are so many opinions out there and gods to choose from!"

PTM: "Good question. There are two basic categories in world religion. In the first category are religions like Hinduism or Buddhism, which are built upon your state of mind. If you just think about life correctly, everything will be fine. The second are works-related religions like Islam, where your good and bad deeds will be weighed at the end of life. It is only with the God of the New Testament that we find, through Jesus, a God who initiates relationship. And it is in this relationship that we find true meaning in life."

Jose

Jose called wanting to hear what kind of message we had, so the PTM shared Jesus as the reality people are seeking. He made this reality possible for us by His death and resurrection, which frees us from the domination of selfishness and sin. Jose agreed with much of what he heard, but he just could not accept that Jesus was actually God. He also questioned why certain books were not included in the Bible. The PTM then described how our Bible was compiled. The church did not decide in the fourth century which books to include in the New Testament, but only confirmed what the church had already accepted as the inspired books.

Jose kept reiterating that he likes Jesus' teaching, but he cannot believe He is divine. He thinks he can believe Jesus' teachings but still not worship Him. The PTM insisted that Jesus is who He said he is, or we can't believe anything He said. "Actually, Jesus is the King of the universe, and He has a kingdom. It's not a matter of being a good person, but of joining or refusing to join His kingdom. Refusing to join amounts to treason, and that will bode badly for you in the future."

As they talked about the kingdom of heaven that Jesus promoted,

Jose identified with the ideals and warmed to this concept of the Gospel. The PTM encouraged him to study the Gospels and the early Anabaptists as an example of people who took this concept seriously. Jose was genuinely intrigued.

After listening to a brief description of the Reformation, Jose responded, "You have to admit Martin Luther was a pretty cool dude."

"Luther did bring some truth to his time, but he also hated the Jews. In fact, Hitler used Luther's antisemitism to justify what he did in the Holocaust. Other reformers like John Calvin burned men at the stake. This doesn't appear to be actions of a redeemed people."

At the conclusion of the call, Jose seemed thankful for the conversation, though he wasn't ready to admit that Jesus was divine. The PTM encouraged Jose to read his Bible. "Jesus promised that those who ask will receive,[n] and the Scriptures promise that faith comes by hearing and hearing by the Word of God."[o]

Benjamin

Benjamin was a congenial caller who seemed open to finding truth. The PTM encouraged him to try reading one chapter a day from the book of Matthew to learn more about Jesus and what He taught. Benjamin said he would like to try that. He was raised Catholic, and his knowledge of Scripture was very limited. He went to church when he was a child, but as an adult he had not read the Bible.

Benjamin was very interested in conserving nature and was particularly concerned about doing anything that might ruin another tree. The PTM offered to send him a Bible since he didn't have one, but he didn't want that. A new Bible would mean another tree might need to be cut down. However, he was interested in finding a second-hand one, so the PTM encouraged him to find one in a local thrift store.

---

[n] Matthew 7:8; Luke 11:9, 10

[o] Romans 10:17

Eventually Benjamin brought up the real reason he had called. He said that sometimes when he passed one of these billboards, his radio would miraculously switch to a Christian station. It happened enough, according to Benjamin, that he felt he had better call. The PTM encouraged him to purchase a Bible, start reading it regularly, and then call back when he had questions.

Jayden

This young man immediately launched into the topic of Satanism. Even though he claimed he wasn't a follower of Satan, he was obviously fascinated with the money, prestige, and power that the powers of darkness offered. The other person in the car seemed to be a Christian who had encouraged Jayden to make the call. The PTM could hear the other person occasionally saying a few words and trying to provide some direction to Jayden. After listening for a while, the PTM shared what the Bible tells us about Satan. He told how Lucifer was cast out of the presence of God and can no longer enter heaven and fight directly against God. He shared that Satan is now determined to kidnap as much of the human race as possible and take them to hell. Sometimes Satan entices men through fame and power.

The PTM mentioned a famous baseball player of years gone by and asked Jayden if he had ever heard of him. Jayden hadn't, and the PTM told him that is how fame is. "Fame is like leaves on a tree—they're beautiful for a time but they all fall off and nobody remembers them anymore. That's how fame works. When you die, you know how much money you are going to take with you? None. Zero. The Scriptures tell us that we come into life naked, and we go out the same way. We will take nothing with us."

The PTM continued by sharing about the power of Jesus Christ, the effect of the new birth on our lives, and how this changes our relationship with God. Jayden wanted to know if he could call back later with more questions, and the call concluded with a sharing of phone numbers and an encouragement for Jayden to read the Word of God for himself.

Amelia

Amelia had seen a billboard proclaiming evidence for God, then she passed another one and decided she was supposed to call. Amelia asked many questions but didn't reveal much about herself. The PTM shared a little about his life, some of the mistakes he had made, and then the blessing of finding forgiveness in Jesus.

Very cautiously, Amelia then began telling a little about her own life. She said she would need to make some lifestyle changes if she was going to follow Jesus. She has a very high-paying job in the entertainment industry and, even as she spoke, was on her way to a casino for a night of revelry. She asked for prayer and then asked if someone could contact her again. Due to the nature of her work, she thought it might be better if a woman called her back. Amelia was a young woman caught up in sexual perversion, yet wanting out and wondering what it would look like to actually follow Jesus.

Noah

Noah, a truck driver, called saying he wants to repent, but feels he has insufficient faith and doesn't know if he can. Before his marriage, he had a son out of wedlock. Noah and his wife have custody of the son, and he is the love of their lives. At one point, he and his wife were separated. During that time, he had another child with another young lady. This woman now wants him to leave his wife for her. She has warned Noah that if he doesn't do this, she will make him pay and do all she can to make his life miserable.

Noah was confused. Should he leave his wife? What is his responsibility to this second child? Noah's parents are divorced. His mother is an atheist, but his father is a believer.

> PTM: "Noah, it is God's will for you to stay with your wife, but you should provide support for the child and pursue as much

contact with the child as possible. But it is also essential that you repent, surrender to Jesus as Lord, be baptized, and live in obedient discipleship."

Noah: "But attending church regularly is impossible. I am always on the road on Sunday because I am a team driver."

PTM: "Could you possibly find a job near home so you could spend more time with your wife and child?"

Noah: "I am trying to earn enough now to make it possible to eventually be at home more."

PTM: "God intends for us to follow Jesus together with other believers. You need the encouragement, teaching, prayers, and accountability you will receive by fellowship with others. You also need the counsel of a pastor for the many decisions you have to make."

Noah: "Because of my sin, I see a lot of pain in my future. Can I expect to ever experience joy again?"

PTM: "Yes. God still cares and wants the best for you. The sorrow for your sin that you are experiencing will deepen your character and keep you aware of your dependence on God. Jesus said that His teachings were given to us so His joy could remain in us and that our joy could be full.[p] If you faithfully follow Jesus, you will again experience joy!"

Harley

Harley had just left a casino when he saw this billboard, and being discouraged, he decided to call. He confessed to being a gambler and said he has been losing a lot of money. "I play poker, and I hate losing more than I enjoy winning. But I can't seem to quit! And lately I have

---

[p] John 15:11

been wondering about the meaning of life."

The PTM took the opportunity to explain that life is intended for us to love and serve God. "We're created by God to have a relationship with Him, and we have a vacuum in our soul that is never quite satisfied when we try to fill it with something besides God."

Harley said he had seven vices, and those vices included women, drugs, booze, and gambling. He didn't say what the other three vices were, but said he indulges in all of them. The PTM shared the Gospel of the kingdom with Harley, explaining the gift of salvation that God has offered to us through Jesus Christ.

> Harley: "Well, I am going to make a valiant effort to change!"
>
> PTM: "Harley, it's not just making a valiant effort. We must be born again through the blood of Jesus Christ."
>
> Harley: "Well, thank you for taking the time to talk with me. You've talked me off the ledge! Thank you for that!"

Harley then hung up, and the PTM wasn't sure what he meant by "talking me off the ledge." It almost sounded as if he had been contemplating suicide, but he didn't say.

Ronnie

Ronnie was a Christian for six years before falling into drugs and alcohol. He now lives with a woman and has two children. He would like a closer walk with God but finds it hard to change. "I just can't seem to surrender!"

The PTM reminded Ronnie of Jesus' promise that everyone who asks receives.[q] "You need to ask God to give you the desire and ability to make a complete surrender to Jesus."

Ronnie said he is a vegan. He finds it very offensive that Christians raise animals in unnatural conditions and brutally slaughter them. The

---

[q] Matthew 7:8

PTM told Ronnie that true Christians respect all of God's creation and treat them with kindness. However, God did give animals to man after the flood to eat, and noted that Jesus ate fish as well. "You must be careful, Ronnie, that your emphasis on the use of animals does not distract your focus from surrender and obedience to Jesus."

Ronnie said he understood, and the PTM spent some time encouraging him to read the Sermon on the Mount and to study the Gospels. He also challenged his fornication. Ronnie said he and his girlfriend are engaged, but the PTM told him he should refrain from marital relations until they are actually married. Ronnie is also opposed to killing humans and doesn't understand why most Christians support war. The PTM explained that many have compromised the teachings of Jesus in this area, and Ronnie was encouraged to know that some Christians oppose war and killing.

5. Morality Issues

Ellis

It was a heartrending story. Ellis introduced himself as more spiritual than a fundamental Christian. "I have been saved but never baptized," he said. "I read the Bible and want to follow Jesus, but I find the reading hard to understand." Seven years ago Ellis divorced his wife. "We married when she was 18 and I was 21. We were very immature but loved each other, and then she started coming home late with suspicious stories about her activities. I tried to forgive her and go on, but finally things got so bad I divorced her. She ran around with another man, got pregnant, had a miscarriage, and ended up in the hospital. I blamed myself for all this and made efforts to restore our relationship. We got together again and began to renew our love. But then she left me, remarried, and now has a child."

He paused for a moment. "I have studied the Gospels about divorce and remarriage and can't decide if I am free to remarry. I want an intimate relationship with a companion so badly, and I feel called to have a family. What do you believe about my situation?"

The PTM told Ellis he feels sorry for him and knows he is in a difficult situation. "Up until modern times, the church viewed divorce as wrong. Of course, people today see this differently, but I don't believe God has ever changed His mind. The Apostle Paul explains Jesus' position on marriage in his letter to the church at Corinth, saying if there is a separation, the spouse is to remain unmarried or be reconciled to the spouse.[r] I know this is a hard saying, and I sympathize with what this means to you, but you asked me to tell you the truth about your situation."

Ellis was very understanding. "I thank you for telling me the truth, but it seems unfair that I must live without a companion because of what I did before I knew the truth. Why does God give me desires that I now can't fulfill? What do I do with those desires?"

The PTM referred Ellis to the book of Matthew, where Jesus said that some people make themselves eunuchs for the kingdom of heaven's sake.[s] "Ellis, what do you think men do with their desires when they are thrown into prison for the rest of their lives? God gives us abundant grace for our crosses when we choose to obey Him."[t]

Ellis seemed very appreciative and said he wanted to do further research. "I don't want to violate the truth, but I want to be sure of the truth on this matter!"

Carter

Carter called wanting to know if it is legalism to obey the Bible. "For example, the Bible says somewhere that women shouldn't teach men. But people say it is legalism to obey teachings like that. What do you think?"

The PTM responded by assuring Carter that following Scriptural

---

[r] 1 Corinthians 7:10, 11

[s] Matthew 19:12

[t] 2 Corinthians 9:8

teaching is not legalism. "It is never legalism to obey Jesus. Jesus told His disciples, 'If you keep my commandments, ye shall abide in my love.'[u] That doesn't sound like legalism. In addition, Jesus said He only did what His Father told Him to do. Did this demean Him? Of course not." The PTM then spoke to Carter about ways the Gospel has been compromised. Many Christians today openly disobey the teachings of Jesus, including His teaching against divorce and remarriage.

This topic hit Carter very hard, and he shared that he is actually divorced and remarried himself. So the PTM read Matthew 19:3-12, sometimes called the "exception clause," and discussed how some use it to permit remarriage after divorce. But it was never understood that way before Erasmus[v] in the 1500s. The PTM tried to help Carter see the devastation this compromise has caused for the church and society.

Carter seemed sobered by this discussion. "My first wife was unfaithful to me. I forgave her, but she left me anyway. Then I remarried with the blessing of my pastor. But if I had known what you just told me, I would have done differently. What shall I do now?"

As they continued talking and looking at various Scriptures, Carter concluded that if what he was hearing is true, he is living in adultery. The PTM encouraged him to open his heart to the truth and study Jesus' teachings on the subject for himself. It was a very sad call from a young man with a fervent passion to be an obedient disciple.

Mason

Mason said he had driven past a sign that asked if he was going to heaven or hell. He was feeling discouraged because of going through a divorce, so he decided to call.

---

[u] John 15:10

[v] Erasmus was a Dutch scholar (1466-1536) who lived during the Reformation. He was critical of the abuses within the Catholic Church and called for reform, but he chose not to join Luther or Calvin. He continued to recognize the authority of the pope while attempting to change the church from within. He remained a member of the Catholic Church all his life.

PTM: "So, Mason, tell me a little about your marriage and why you are getting a divorce."

Mason: "My wife and I were married when we were 23. We're 35 now, so we've been together about twelve years. We haven't been happy together for quite a while, so we have been working on this divorce for the last ten months or so. Actually, it is scheduled to be finalized tomorrow morning."

PTM: "Does your wife want to get divorced?"

Mason: "Well, no, she wanted to stay together, but I haven't been happy with her for quite a while."

PTM: "Mason, were either of you involved in unfaithfulness or pornography?"

There was silence on the line for a moment.

Mason: "Yes, I did have a problem with pornography, and I have also been involved with another woman."

PTM: "Well, Mason, you need to understand what God thinks about this issue, and what Jesus said about divorce and remarriage. The woman you are still married to for the next twelve hours or so is your true wife. God honors that marriage, and He wants you to be true to it. According to the Bible, if you get divorced, you don't have the option of getting married to someone else."

Understandably, this hit Mason very hard. He didn't know the Bible taught this, but he felt his situation was a little different. He felt that his marriage had been arranged, that he had been urged to marry this woman, and it had turned out that he wasn't pleased with her. Mason said he wasn't happy in this marriage because his wife didn't want to do the same things he enjoyed and go places he wanted to go.

PTM: "It sounds like there is a possibility that your wife would agree to stay with you if you would have a change of heart. I would really encourage you to reconsider!"

Mason: "So you are saying if I do get divorced I have to stay single? And if I do get married again, then I am not going to heaven?"

PTM: "That is how I understand the Bible. The road to eternal life is not an easy road; it's not the easy decision. I would encourage you to choose life. There are other decisions that might be easier in the short term, but they lead to death."

Mason: "But it seems I'm in a lose-lose situation."

PTM: "In a sense you are. You're going to either lose your eternal life, or you're going to lose some of those pleasures of sin that you've been chasing. I would urge you to lose the sin and choose life."

Mason: "Wow, I'm going to have to pray about this!"

PTM: "Yes, Mason, I would urge you to pray, but then you must also choose to obey and honor God. Often when people choose to honor God, He in turn honors them. When they honor the commitment they made in marriage, God will sometimes put new love back into that marriage. Right now you say there is no love. But when you married your wife, you made a commitment to her, and God still honors that commitment."

Leah

Leah said she has been a Christian since 1979, and she called because she is troubled by the activities her husband is involved in. She is 67 years old and was returning from visiting some of her children when she saw a sign and thought she would call. Leah thinks her husband is a Christian, but he spends a lot of money on cigars and beer, and that bothers her. So the PTM asked a little more about her life, and it became evident that the children she had been visiting were from a previous marriage.

PTM: "Leah, were you married before you married your husband?"

Leah: "Yes, my first husband was unfaithful and left me for another woman. But even though my first husband isn't a believer, he has stayed with the same woman for 26 years since he married her. So I am glad about that."

PTM: "Are you aware of what Jesus said about divorce and remarriage? He said that anyone who puts away his wife and marries another commits adultery. And if a woman puts her husband away and marries another man, she is committing adultery as well."[w]

Leah: "Yes, I know the Bible talks about adultery and says it is a sin, and I repented of that years ago."

PTM: "But as I would understand it, as long as you continue in this adulterous relationship you are living in a state of continual sin."

Leah was genuinely shocked, and this was obviously a blow to her. The PTM spoke gently to her about adultery, emphasizing the teachings of Jesus and going to 1 Corinthians 6:9-10. He told her that regardless of what society around us says, adultery is sin and will bar individuals from heaven unless they repent and abandon it. Leah seemed to be carefully listening, and before hanging up the PTM prayed with her and encouraged her to discuss this with her husband and seek God's will for their future.

---

[w] Mark 10:11, 12

Daniel

Daniel's very first question was, "Is marriage for life?"

"Yes, it certainly is," the PTM responded and then quoted several verses that support this conclusion.

> Daniel: "Wow! This is just a confirmation. My wife and I were married a number of years ago. We have two children and it was the first marriage for both of us. I wasn't saved at the time, I made some mistakes, and now we are separated. However, I would like to get back together, but she doesn't seem too interested. She says that God told her to stay divorced. I also suspect she is pursuing another relationship."
>
> PTM: "Regardless what she says, Daniel, divorce is not God's will."
>
> Daniel: "I don't think God wants us to be divorced either, but I have talked to a number of Christians, and even church leaders about this, and they tell me to move on with my life and find a different wife."
>
> PTM: "Daniel, I would urge you not to get married again. Further, I would encourage you to tell your wife that you are committed to her, and even if she doesn't return, you will remain single as long as she is alive. I would also strongly recommend that you not put pressure on her but show kindness in every way possible. You should also show contrition for the sins of the past and continue to be faithful in providing for her and the children."
>
> Daniel: "Thank you so much for confirming what I had been suspecting!"

Albert

This was a very emotional call, and Albert was looking for comfort. The conversation had just started when Albert explained that his "husband" had just left him. The PTM immediately recognized that this had been a homosexual union, but as the call continued, things got even stranger. Albert said his partner wanted to regender himself and become a woman. Albert had assumed his partner was satisfied with their relationship, so the separation was painful for him.

The PTM went to the Word of God and talked of God's holiness and of His desire for a holy people. Eventually they worked their way through the need for redemption and the salvation provided through Jesus Christ. The PTM mentioned 1 Corinthians 6:9-11, but he didn't read it to Albert. Rather, he asked Albert to write down the reference and then read it for himself after the call. The PTM really wanted Albert to discover for himself what the Bible says about sexual sin and how God sees it. He also wanted him to know that deliverance is possible.

"Albert, when you read this passage, you will find it is about a group of people in a city called Corinth. These were people who had been involved in all kinds of sins, but their lives had been transformed and changed by the power of Jesus Christ. This is available to anyone who will submit their life to Jesus Christ."

Abigail

Abigail said she was calling because she wanted to know the truth. The PTM told her that all of us want truth, and when we search for truth we are really looking for reality. He shared some evidences for God and then spoke of what the Bible says about our sinfulness and of the fact that Jesus came to deal with our sin problem.

> Abigail: "I don't think you like me."
>
> PTM: "Why wouldn't I like you?"
>
> Abigail: "Um, because I am a lesbian, and I believe it goes against everything God wants for me."
>
> PTM: "So, Abigail, have you been finding peace in your life?"

Abigail: "No, not lately, to be honest. It's been really stressful with my parents. I go to school and I'm always stressed out."

PTM: "Did you know that Jesus is willing to be there for us?"

Abigail: "I don't think He has been there for me lately."

PTM: "Do you have a Bible?"

Abigail: "Yes."

PTM: "Abigail, here is what I want you to do. Take your Bible and start reading in the book of Matthew. As you read, give thought to who Jesus is, what He did, and what He wants to do for us. Can you do that?"

Abigail: "Yes, I can."

PTM: "It is so easy for us to lose perspective. At times we need to pick up our Bibles and regain the reality that God is in control. Since God is in control and cares about us, we have a purpose for living."

Abigail: "So God doesn't hate me because I am a lesbian?"

PTM: "God created each one of us and cares about each one of us. We arc all sinners, and the cross is about forgiveness. You are just as valuable as anyone else on the face of this earth."

Abigail: "You know, you are the first person to ever tell me that."

PTM: "Each one of us is a sinner by nature, and each one of us has broken our relationship with God. The reason people fail to find peace with God is because they refuse to turn away from their sin."

The PTM continued to speak of the need for holiness in our lives. He then prayed with her and gave her his number if she had more questions. Abigail seemed thankful for the discussion and the encouragement.

Louis

Louis called saying he has been having a very difficult day. He has been in a relationship with another man for seven years. He has been married to him now for three years, but his partner is becoming increasingly violent. Sometimes he's nice, but at other times he can be very angry and even dangerous. Several times he has been so violent that Louis has pulled a gun on him and told him to calm down.

> Louis: "But I'm not that kind of person. I don't want to hurt my partner. So I'm, like, up against a wall, in a sense, because I don't want to call the police. If the police come, he will be very nice, very sweet, and very gentle until they leave; then he'll just explode. I'm really becoming afraid of him."

Louis is 66 years old. As a young man, he went to church, became a member, and was involved in missions. But he knows he has somehow gone astray, and now he is very distraught and looking for answers. "I'm a level-headed man, but I just don't know what to do. I know I've made some wrong choices."

> PTM: "Louis, are you ready to make choices that will help you return to that relationship you had with Jesus Christ and God? Or how do you feel about that?"

> Louis: "Yes, that's what I want to do."

> PTM: "You can go ahead and pray right now if you are ready."

> Louis: "God, I'm sorry for what I've done. I want to hear your voice. I just want to hear your voice! You know, I used to help people like me. I used to reach out and help those around me who were broken and living in sin. And now here I am in this place. I don't want to be here."

Louis seemed very sincere and remorseful. After he had finished praying, the PTM asked if he would like someone to contact him or have a meeting to assist him in turning his life over to God. "Yes, I need somebody to talk to, but I'm so embarrassed about my lifestyle."

Louis has a good job, but he is concerned about separating from his partner. "I'm afraid to just kick the guy out because I'm not sure what he would do to me."

The PTM told Louis about a man he has worked with during the past couple years who is in a similar situation, and assured him there is hope. "God does love you intensely, Louis. He wants the best for you. You need to pursue God with all your heart, and God will provide and take care of you."

Finn

This young man said he had a question. "Should same-sex couples refrain from sexual activity until after they're married?"

> PTM: "First of all, you need to understand God's original intent. From the very beginning God made humans male and female, and designed them to live together in close relationship for life."[x]
>
> Finn: "That's not my question."
>
> PTM: "But it's important, when answering questions like this, that we go back and see what the original plan for humanity was. Here in America it is perfectly legal for two consenting adults to have sex outside of marriage. But that's not what God says. God says that a fornicator cannot inherit the kingdom of God. When life is over, we won't be judged by the United States government—it's the Word of God that's going to judge us."
>
> Finn: "Well, you're not really answering my question. So what

---

[x] Matthew 19:4-6

about transgender? Is there anything wrong with someone changing their gender?

PTM: "Well, suppose the artist of the Mona Lisa would have given me that expensive portrait, and I would decide to paint a beard on it. He is the artist, and I would be messing up his expertise and ruining the portrait. In the case of humanity, changing my gender would be destroying the purpose God had in mind for my life. And think about this, Finn—regardless how many operations or hormone treatments I receive, it will not change the fact that every cell in my body still has the male gene in it. It's there, and I can't get around it. It is important that we honor the Creator for who He is and for what He has done in creation."

Evelyn

Evelyn immediately identified herself as gay and an atheist. Since she had been so forthcoming about her life, the PTM began sharing a little about his. He told what it was like growing up in a Christian home, included a few Bible stories in his narrative, and then shared how following Jesus has changed him. Evelyn was intrigued and very interested. She was also fascinated by how the PTM had responded to her statement that she was gay and an atheist. "Whenever I tell Christians who and what I am, their immediate response is, 'Well, if you're lesbian, you're going to hell.' "

PTM: "Evelyn, all of us have a sinful nature, which puts all of us on the road to hell. Until we're born again by the Spirit of God, life really goes downhill. But when we become a child of God, He gives us a divine nature that supersedes our sinful nature and begins subduing and conquering that sinful nature. God wants to empower us to live a holy life."

The PTM could tell that Evelyn was intrigued, so he continued. "You know, I used to be a school teacher, and I loved giving assignments. Could I give you an assignment?"

Evelyn: "Sure."

PTM: "I would like for you to read the book of Matthew in the Bible, while asking this question: 'Who is Jesus?' Then, after you are finished, ask whether Jesus is real or not. Can you do that?"

Evelyn: "Yes, I can."

PTM: "Now, you know, a good teacher always has a report card, right? So when you are finished with your assignment, I want you to give me a call. I want to hear what you have to say."

Evelyn agreed, and the PTM asked if he could pray for her before they disconnected. Evelyn said that would be fine. "I'm driving in the rain right now, so remember to pray for that."

The PTM enjoyed the irony of having an atheist ask him to pray for her safety!

Jackson

Jackson: "Just so you understand me, you need to understand that I'm on testosterone and I'm transgender."

PTM: "Have you already had surgery for that purpose?"

Jackson: "Yes, why do you ask?"

PTM: "I was hoping you hadn't already had a surgery that is irreversible."

Jackson: "But homosexuality harms nobody."

PTM: "It may seem that way, but man's judgments about the effects of something can't always be trusted. The Bible tells us that there is a way that seems right to man, but the end of that road are the ways of death."[y]

---

[y] Proverbs 14:12

Jackson: "What does that mean?"

PTM: "Let me illustrate it this way. When I was young, almost no one was divorced and remarried. But it seemed reasonable that if people who were unhappily married would divorce and marry better partners, then everybody would be in a better situation, including the children. So people ignored what God said in the Bible. If a marriage wasn't going well, people divorced their spouses and married someone else. But today people are discovering that this wasn't a good idea. This has been devastating to homes and children, but now it's too late. We can't put the toothpaste back in the tube. God's laws are not arbitrary, but based on His knowledge of how He created man and what is best for him."

Jackson: "But I don't see why man needs a God to be moral and do what is right. Why can't men just come up with a collective morality that is wholesome and works for everyone?"

PTM: "Well, that was the argument in Nazi Germany. We tend to use clever rationalizations, but even our best intentions are overcome with selfishness."

The PTM then described the kingdom of heaven and God's desire that we live in peace and harmony. Jackson assumed he was speaking of the afterlife and began to object. But the PTM assured him that God intends for mankind to live in tranquility now, and the kingdom of heaven on earth actually fulfills the ideals we carry in our hearts.

"But Jackson, this will never occur unless man's selfishness is dealt with, and Jesus Christ is the only one who can free us from our self-centeredness. I would encourage you to repent, surrender to Jesus as Lord and Master, and let Jesus make you into the person God intended for you to be!"

At the end of the conversation, Jackson seemed intrigued and interested in learning more.

6. Religious Confusion

Thomas

Raised in an evangelical Christian home, Thomas later converted to Catholicism. He seemed to have reacted to the harshness of Calvinistic predestination and the laxity of morals among the evangelicals he knew. After sharing his past, Thomas had a question. "What do you believe about purgatory?"

> PTM: "Those who teach and believe in purgatory do not understand God's dealings with men. They believe that if a person's confessions of sin are not up-to-date when he dies, he cannot enter heaven. However, the Bible says that a person who is truly walking in the light never comes into condemnation.[z] It also tells us that a person who is walking in the light of Jesus is kept clean by His blood.[aa] The key to our position with God is a relationship of passionate obedience to Christ. But Thomas, you can't play games with this wonderful truth. If you presume upon it and become careless about sin, then you are not walking in the light, and this cleansing doesn't apply."

> Thomas: "Interesting! I have never heard it explained like that. So what about all the people who die and have never heard about Jesus? What will happen to them in the final judgment? I tend to believe that God will eventually reconcile everyone. What do you think?"

> PTM: "The Bible doesn't tell us that everyone will eventually be saved, and we shouldn't hold that sort of hope out to people. However, God is the judge, and He hasn't told us everything. We can be confident that God will be equitable in His

---

[z] Romans 8:1

[aa] 1 John 1:7

judgment in all situations."

Thomas: "So what do think about the Apostle's Creed?"

PTM: "I agree with what it says. It's what it does not say that is disappointing. It says nothing about the kingdom of God, but focuses primarily on a 'save me' concept of the Gospel. My goal as a believer is not just getting to heaven, but living out God's will here on earth. To be a part of God's kingdom."

As the conversation continued, Thomas could see that God's purpose is much greater than just keeping people out of hell. He seemed excited that God has a goal of placing His ideals on display to a watching world. In the end he asked for more information and wanted to stay in contact.

Aaron

Aaron was a young man who just wanted to know what we were telling people. So the PTM presented Jesus as the truth—the reality of true humanity. Aaron wanted to know if we believe we are saved by our works.

PTM: "No, we are not saved by our works. However, the Bible says that a follower of Jesus will be obedient to Him and that obedience is very important. In fact, at the end of the New Testament, in the book of Revelation, the writer says, 'Blessed are they that do his commandments, that they may have right to the tree of life, and may enter in through the gates into the city.'[ab] So it appears that what we do in this life will matter in the judgment."

Aaron: "Well, my pastor, who understands both Greek and Hebrew, says that verses like that are talking about special

---

[ab] Revelation 22:14

rewards we will receive in heaven. My pastor says that the Greek explains so many things that are not obvious in our English Bibles."

PTM: "Well, we need to be careful in interpreting the Bible. This Scripture reflects the clear teaching of many other Scriptures. Jesus said many will say 'Lord, Lord,' and He will tell them to depart from Him because they didn't *do* the will of His Father."

Aaron: "So what about men like David? He sinned and suffered for his sin, but he didn't lose his relationship with God."

PTM: "God was willing to forgive David because he repented of his sin. However, if David hadn't repented, I don't believe God would have forgiven him, and he would have been separated from God."

Aaron: "But you don't believe you can lose your salvation, do you?"

PTM: "Yes, we are clearly told in the Bible that we can drift away from God. The book of Hebrews warns believers about this."

Aaron: "That's terrible. That must be awful to live in fear that you will lose your salvation."

PTM: "I do not live in fear because we are told that His seed remains in us and will not freely let us walk in sin.[ac] But we can choose to ignore the Spirit's powerful promptings and drift away."

Jacob

Jacob said he had been raised in the church and his grandfather was a preacher. "But it wasn't for me. I never received any answers to prayer or saw any evidence of God doing anything."

[ac] 1 John 3:9

PTM: "Christianity isn't about focusing on what God will do for me. Rather, it is responding to God regardless if I see results in this life or not. True Christians find their delight in pleasing God no matter what is happening in their lives."

Jacob: "Really, I'm a pretty good person, so I think when I stand before God I can make a pretty good case."

PTM: "But Jacob, what we consider good is usually rationalized selfishness. The Bible says there is a way that seems good to a man, but the end thereof are the ways of death.[ad] For example, let's just say a young man wants to live with his girlfriend even though they aren't married. He can convince himself that this is right, simply because he loves her and treats her kindly."

Jacob: "Well, actually, I am living with my girlfriend right now."

PTM: "God requires repentance and total surrender before we can enter His kingdom. It's like a surgeon. Before he can start working, that patient has to crawl up on the operating table and totally surrender himself to the surgeon. The patient knows that the surgeon is going to cut and that it will hurt. But he also knows that the surgeon has his good in mind. That is what God requires of us, and if we aren't willing to completely surrender control to Him, He can't work on us."

Jacob: "So what if I wait till the end of life to surrender to God?"

PTM: "A person who expects to do that is presuming on God's mercy. He's trying to have his own way and heaven too. The person who keeps sinning is hardening his heart, and it is not at all certain he will even want to repent in the end. We make our decisions, and then our decisions make us."

[ad] Proverbs 14:12

At the end of the conversation, Jacob still wasn't sure if Christianity was for him, but he wanted to give it more thought.

Ezra

Ezra grew up Jewish and has always been confused about how Christ's sacrifice could atone for someone else's sins. After all, when we sin, we are the only ones who can make things right.

The PTM tried to explain that sin isn't just against others, it is ultimately against God. "As Joseph said to Potiphar's wife, our sin is not only against others but also against God. Jesus was the perfect sacrifice, and only the sacrifice of perfect blood could expunge our sin from the record."

Ezra was very congenial during the discussion, but he said this concept just doesn't make sense to him.

So the PTM took him back to the sacrifices of his own people. Sacrifices were all through the Old Law, but Ezra said that had never made any sense to him either. It soon became obvious that Ezra takes a very rationalistic approach to the Biblical record. As they continued to talk, Ezra said he doubts the veracity of the creation story, the account of Noah's flood, and many other Biblical accounts. So they spoke for a while about the reliability of the Bible, and specifically the accuracy of the Gospel accounts. Ezra was fascinated when he heard of Jesus' kingdom. This seemed to be a new concept for him, and he found the idea of Jesus promoting an equitable society compelling.

But Ezra wasn't ready to surrender to Jesus yet. He wanted to keep searching. "I haven't made a religion out of unbelief, and I am still seeking with an open mind. Thank you for the challenges you have given me during this conversation!"

Just as the call was concluding, Ezra said his wife had just told him they were running low on gas and he needed to refocus his attention on his driving. He chuckled as he concluded. "But maybe my wife and I are running out of spiritual gas, and this conversation might be crucial to the saving of our souls."

William

William was a Church of Christ pastor and called with a question about water baptism. He said he had asked fifty people whether baptism is necessary, and forty-eight of them said it wasn't. So he wanted to know what we thought.

The PTM quoted Mark 16:16 and Matthew 28:19, noting that baptism is a clear command of Jesus. "An evidence that a person has surrendered to Jesus as his Lord and Master is his passion to obey everything Jesus says. So a follower of Jesus would want to be baptized." They discussed scenarios where people believe but die before they can be baptized, and both agreed that God would honor their faith as He did for the thief on the cross. The PTM then changed the subject. "Are you aware that the Church of Christ at its beginning was nonresistant?"

> William: "Yes, and our church held that position through World War I and up to World War II."
>
> PTM: "So why did you discard this belief and practice? Jesus was very clear on this teaching."

William was a little vague in his response but said he does believe in nonresistance. The PTM concluded by encouraging him to teach this doctrine to his people.

Lucy

Lucy has been a police officer for the past ten years and has seen a lot of evil. She called wondering why God allows so much suffering in the world.

> PTM: "We don't always know why God allows the things that He does. But consider this: God could have created us as robots that always do His will and never do anything wrong. But that would have left us without the possibility of an authentic relationship with Him or others. I don't see how God could have created us

with the possibility of relationships without giving us the gift of choice. And with choice comes the possibility of bad choices, and this usually causes someone to suffer. Often innocent people."

Lucy: "This doesn't really answer my question. If God is good and all-powerful, why not come up with a different plan that doesn't result in so much suffering?"

PTM: "You are right; I haven't completely answered your question. In fact, no religion has ever completely answered the question. But most recognize that suffering is necessary for strong character development. As Christians, we see enough positive perspective for suffering to trust God even when we don't understand His larger perspective."

Lucy: "That makes sense. As a police officer, I face the possibility of someday using lethal force to save the lives of others. What do you think about that?"

The PTM explained the two kingdoms and how God has removed the sword from Christians so the church can demonstrate the love of God. He affirmed the need for control by government to keep order, but explained God's kingdom as a separate kingdom that demonstrates what the world would be like if everyone followed Jesus.

PTM: "Lucy, suppose that a thousand years ago the Christians who took the Gospel to Russia would have taught Jesus' commands against the use of the sword and the accumulation of wealth. The Marxists would have had no situation to correct, nothing to react against, and 100,000,000 lives would have been saved. But instead, the church took a 'gospel' to Russia with some of the most important parts missing. In many ways, the church, which God established to be the solution to much of the world's suffering, is now part of the problem instead of the solution God intended."

Rachel

Rachel: "Hi, I have seen your billboards and I got the number because I have some questions. I have some friends who are believers in Jesus. I'm Jewish and believe in the Torah,[ae] but I have some doubts. The reason I am calling is that my friends who believe in Jesus seem so happy, and I want to know why. So I'm calling just to get some information."

PTM: "Sure, I would be glad to help however I can. First, understand that I also believe in the Torah. But I believe in more than just the Torah. God called Abraham and gave him a son of promise. All of this pointed forward to a Son of promise who was going to come from God. Then, for 1,500 years, God dealt with the people of Israel. You are familiar with the Passover, aren't you?"

Rachel: "Of course. We were taught about the Passover from little up."

PTM: "Rachel, the Passover lamb was given to demonstrate how Jesus Christ would come and be killed to deliver us from our sins. That is why Jesus is described as the Lamb of God that takes away the sin of the world.[af] His blood has the power to take our sins away so we can stand before God cleansed and forgiven. When we have been cleansed by His blood, God can implant His Holy Spirit within us, and that is what transforms us into a true child of God. This is available for Jew or Gentile—anyone who will believe. Moses said a long time ago, 'A prophet shall the Lord your God raise up unto you of your brethren, like unto me; him shall ye hear,'[ag] and he was speaking

---

[ae] The Torah is the law of God as revealed to Moses and recorded in the first five books of the Bible. Sometimes it is referred to as the Pentateuch.

[af] John 1:29

[ag] Acts 3:22

about Jesus Christ."

Rachel: "But I thought that was talking about Joshua."

PTM: "Well, in many of these prophesies there is often a dual purpose. Did you realize that the name Joshua in Hebrew is Jesus in Greek?"

Rachel: "No I didn't know that, I will need to look that up. But I am at my destination now. Thank you for taking time to talk to me."

Esther

Esther was traveling with her Christian friend and having a religious discussion when they saw the billboard. Esther felt somehow responsible for the crucifixion and called asking if she was going to hell because she is Jewish.

Esther: "I feel guilty because my people killed Jesus!"

PTM: "Esther, the Roman soldiers did the killing, and the Jews were no guiltier than the rest of humanity for His death. It was the sins of all of us that put Him on that cross. You should not be feeling guilty for the sins of others, but for your own sins. Instead, I would encourage you to investigate the evidences for Jesus' resurrection. That is the basis for the Christian faith."

Esther: "I sometimes think I should be a Catholic, then I could go and confess my sin and get rid of my guilt."

PTM: "It's not just a matter of dealing with one sin in our lives. God calls us to repent of all our sins and surrender to Jesus as our Lord and Master. God wants all of our life, not just one part of it. God wants us to experience a joyful, guilt-free life, but we cannot experience that life until we are freed from the selfishness and sin that controls us. In some way, Jesus' death and resurrection frees us. If we totally surrender to Jesus, we will experience forgiveness and freedom from the power of sin and be able to live a life of Christlikeness by the power of the Holy Spirit that God gives us."

Esther seemed to understand the message. She also revealed that she is in a lesbian relationship. The PTM urged her to get a copy of the New Testament and let Jesus speak for Himself. Before they disconnected she agreed to do that.

Frank

Frank's first question was about the Trinity. Frank's wife was raised Mormon and was taught that God, Jesus, and the Holy Spirit are not one person but three separate personalities. After discussing this, Frank wanted some advice regarding divorce and remarriage. He had questions about the "exception clause"[ah] and wondered if remarriage was acceptable in some situations. Frank said he is in a difficult marriage and is trying to determine the best route.

After some explanation about this passage, the PTM noted that whatever we conclude, it is obvious that the disciples didn't understand Jesus as allowing remarriage, because their immediate response was, "If marriage is like that, it's better not to get married!"[ai]

The discussion then turned to Mormonism. The PTM recommended some literature, and then Frank shared a question he had been pondering. "My in-laws are Mormons, and they say they have such peace. If they are wrong, how can that be?"

> PTM: "Frank, our feelings are not the arbiters of what is true. I talk to many atheists who say they have so much more peace now that they have rejected Christianity. Truth is determined by whether it harmonizes with what Jesus lived and taught."

[ah] Matthew 5:32; 19:9

[ai] Matthew 19:10

Frank then wanted to know about infant baptism, and the PTM addressed the meaning of baptism and why only believers should be baptized. He described the history of the Anabaptists and encouraged Frank to do more research. Frank said he is not a member of a church and has not been able to find a church that fits what he is learning about the Gospel. "For the past six months, I have been studying the Bible intensely."

> PTM: "Frank, I would encourage you to find a church that obeys all of Jesus' teachings, especially His teachings on divorce and remarriage and nonresistance. You need a fellowship of believers to surround you with encouragement, counsel, accountability, instruction, and prayer. God never meant for us to live the Gospel on our own but in a fellowship of believers."

Tyler

Tyler started out by asking how the PTM got this job and then moved into the topic of whether baptism is essential for salvation. When Tyler called, the Caller ID had read "Church of the Latter Day Saints," so the PTM knew he was talking to someone from the Mormon church. But as the discussion continued, Tyler seemed unwilling to reveal the fact that he was a Mormon. So finally the PTM decided to address this issue.

> PTM: "Tyler, when you called, my Caller ID said 'Church of the Latter Day Saints.' Why haven't you been honest about who you are?" Tyler apologized, and then the PTM continued. "This has happened repeatedly, and I would like to know why the Mormons are so uncomfortable telling the truth. We get many calls from Mormons who try to pretend they are not. Why is this?"

> Tyler: "I suppose it is because we don't feel accepted by the Christian community, and we desperately want acceptance."

PTM: "But it concerns me that your people can lie without feeling convicted."

This discussion continued for some time, ranging from the difference between the Jesus in the book of Mormon and the Jesus of the Bible, to how atonement takes place. In the end, Tyler was still very confident that the Book of Mormon is just as important as the Bible.

Asad

Asad assumed this was a Muslim hotline, and after discovering it wasn't, wanted to know why anyone would be a Christian.

The PTM explained that the Gospel of Jesus Christ offers a Redeemer, not just a lawgiver who expects us to pull ourselves up by our own bootstraps. "God is a holy God. We can meet Him in peace only if there is no sin on our record, and only Jesus can take away our sins and give us a clean slate and the power to write a new life on it."

Asad: "So what do you think 'jihad' means?"

PTM: "Well, my Muslim friends try to make me believe that jihad is just one's personal struggle, but the Quran is clear that jihad means death to the infidel."

Asad didn't argue with this, but insisted that people shouldn't reject the Quran until they have read it for themselves.

The PTM thanked him for his thoughts, but told him that he had found reality and hope in the Gospel of Jesus Christ, and encouraged Asad to read the Gospels for himself.

Matthew

Matthew began with a question. "Why was Lucifer banished to hell?"

PTM: "The Bible says that Lucifer had natural beauty, but he also had a rebellious spirit and wanted to elevate himself to being God's equal. He had lived in a perfect environment, but when pride was found in him he was cast out of heaven."

Matthew: "Wow. Thank you for explaining that!"

PTM: "Are you a Bible reader, Matthew?"

Matthew: "No."

PTM: "So . . . you don't read the Bible and yet you know Lucifer was banished to hell. How is that?"

Matthew: "Well, I'm a bit of a Satanist."

PTM: "Now that's interesting! I didn't know anyone could be a BIT of a Satanist."

There was a brief pause and then a chuckle. "Actually, I'm more than a BIT of a Satanist."

PTM: "Well, thank you for being truthful about that. You know, that's not like Lucifer. The Bible tells us that he's a liar and the father of lies. I don't think you want to follow someone like that."

Matthew: "Well, I've learned that nothing matters."

PTM: "Matthew, I used to think that way too."

The PTM then shared a brief account of his own conversion and the change that Jesus has made in his life. "When a man finds Jesus, he has hope, and then things do matter. I would encourage you to read the Bible for yourself."

Matthew seemed receptive to this, and before the call was terminated the PTM offered to pray for him, but Matthew wasn't sure about that. "I don't know any prayers."

PTM: "That's okay, Matthew. I'll pray and you can listen."

Bobby

Bobby wanted to know how we can get away with putting up our offensive Christian billboards when he can't get permission from the locals to put up his Norse pagan billboards. The PTM told him he was certain he could exercise the same freedom that we enjoy.

Bobby said his Roman Catholic mother had tried to force her Roman Catholicism down his throat, but he has chosen to worship Norse gods such as Odin. "With the Norse gods, I can be a god among them. They don't require me to be subservient."

The PTM talked with Bobby about the jealousy and violence of those Norse gods, contrasting them to the nonviolence of Jesus' way. Bobby seemed to be intrigued with nonresistance. "I appreciate what you describe, but I probably stand somewhere between nonresistance and violence. I want to live in peace with others, but if they want to fight, I will make it worse for them than they make it for me."

The PTM described ideals of God's kingdom, the fact that God wants His creation to live in harmony, and the reality that selfishness destroys those ideals. Only Jesus can deliver us from selfishness so those ideals can be realized. The conversation seemed to mellow Bobby's original defiance, and at the end he allowed the PTM to pray for him.

Lisa

She called expecting to get upbraided for not being a Christian, and assuming she would be hated by whoever answered the phone. That was simply Lisa's picture of Christianity from what she had observed. When she passed a billboard asking "Where are you going, heaven or hell?" she called to inquire.

Lisa is a practicing Buddhist, loves life, and was a very friendly caller. She was certain that she was opposed to Christianity and freely expressed her concerns. She referenced morality issues with Catholic priests and wondered how people can think Christianity is a good religion with all that going on. And then there were the Crusades. Slaughtering people in the name of God? As a Buddhist, she is opposed to killing any living being. Why would anyone want to be associated with a religion that goes out and kills people?

The PTM then described some of the teachings of Jesus, shared a little on church history, and explained that many Christians throughout history have been opposed to bloodshed. Lisa was genuinely intrigued and confessed she had never heard anything like this before. She then asked a beautiful question. "Well, what does the life of a true Christian look like then?"

This was a tremendous opportunity for the PTM, and he tried to make the best of it. He described the kingdom of Jesus Christ, went through some of His teachings, and concluded by describing how the world today would look if everyone would proclaim Jesus as Lord of their lives. He shared some of the ways true believers try to assist those in need. "Where there's a tornado, we go and try to help rebuild. Where there's hunger, we're there to offer food. True believers have a deep desire to follow Jesus and to bless people, regardless who they are. They aren't trying to be out in front. But know this. All around the globe, followers of Jesus are quietly attempting to bless their communities and share the love of Christ." The PTM challenged Lisa to investigate Jesus for herself and invited her to start reading the Gospels.

This compelling explanation seemed to move Lisa. This wasn't the Christianity she had called to refute, and before hanging up she observed, "The rest of the Christians in America should adopt your belief!"

Endnotes

[1] Jana Reiss, "Religion Declining in Importance for Many Americans, Especially Millennials," Religion News Service, December 10, 2018, <https://religionnews.com/2018/12/10/religion-declining-in-importance-for-many-americans-especially-for-millennials/>, accessed on 7/31/19.

[2] Michael Lipka, "Why America's 'Nones' Left Religion Behind," Pew Research Center, August 24, 2016, <https://www.pewresearch.org/fact-tank/2016/08/24/why-americas-nones-left-religion-behind/>, accessed on 7/31/19.

[3] Blaise Pascal, Blaise Pascal's Pensees, Penguin Books, NY, 1966, p. 75, originally Pensées, 1670, VII (425). Pascal's actual quote was: "What else does this craving, and this helplessness, proclaim but that there was once in man a true happiness, of which all that now remains is the empty print and trace? This he tries in vain to fill with everything around him, seeking in things that are not there the help he cannot find in those that are, though none can help, since this infinite abyss can be filled only with an infinite and immutable object; in other words by God himself."

[4] David Zahl, *Seculosity,* Fortress Press, Minneapolis, MN, 2019, p. xiv.

[5] Capstone Advisory Group, May 4, 2018, <https://www.capstoneadvgroup.com/articles/worlds-largest-consumer-markets---global-commerce>, accessed on 8/3/19.

[6] D.A. Carson, *The Intolerance of Tolerance,* William B. Eerdmans Publishing Company, Grand Rapids, MI, 2012, p. 12.

[7] Dr. Gary Gilley, *This Little Church Went to Market,* Evangelical Press, Darlington, UK, 2005.

[8] Lea Winerman, "By the Numbers: Antidepressant Use on the Rise," American Psychological Association, November 2017, Vol. 48, No. 10, <https://www.apa.org/monitor/2017/11/numbers>, accessed on 8/16/19.

[9] Don Richardson, *Peace Child,* Regal Books, Ventura, CA, 2005.

[10] Harold Pinter, Nobel Lecture, NobelPrize.org., <https://www.nobelprize.org/prizes/literature/2005/pinter/25621-harold-pinter-nobel-lecture-2005/>, accessed on 8/22/19.

[11] Hannah Hartig, "Republicans Turn More Negative Toward Refugees as Number Admitted to U.S. Plummets," Pew Research Center, May 24, 2018, <https://www.pewresearch.org/fact-tank/2018/05/24/republicans-turn-more-negative-toward-refugees-as-number-admitted-to-u-s-plummets/>, accessed on 8/23/19.

[12] Timothy Egan, "Why People Hate Religion," *New York Times,* August 30, 2019, <https://www.nytimes.com/2019/08/30/opinion/trump-religion.html>, accessed on 8/31/19.

[13] World Population Review, <http://worldpopulationreview.com/countries/military-spending-by-country/>, accessed on 8/23/19.

[14] Joseph H. Hellerman, *When the Church Was a Family,* B & H Publishing, Nashville, TN, 2009, p. 67.

[15] C.S. Lewis, *The Problem of Pain,* Collier Books, NY, 1962 Edition, p. 93.

[16] Rahm Emanuel, Interview with the *Wall Street Journal,* November 19, 2008, <https://www.bing.com/videos/search?q=Rahm+Emanuel+interview+with+WSJ&view=detail&mid=46045021855BB9AC302746045021855B-B9AC3027&FORM=VIRE>, accessed on 10/17/19.

[17] Rosaria Butterfield, *The Gospel Comes with a House Key,* Crossway Publishing, Wheaton, IL, 2018, p. 47.

[18] Rosaria Butterfield, *The Secret Thoughts of an Unlikely Convert*, Crown and Covenant Publications, Pittsburgh, PA, 2012.

[19] Butterfield, *The Gospel Comes with a House Key.*

[20] Gary Miller, *It's Not Your Business*, TGS International, Berlin, OH, 2015.

[21] Jack Jenkins, "Nones Now as Big as Evangelicals, Catholics in the US," Religion News Service, March 21, 2019. <https://religionnews.com/2019/03/21/nones-now-as-big-as-evangelicals-catholics-in-the-us/>, accessed on 11/14/19.

[22] Megan Brenan, "40% of Americans Believe in Creationism," Gallup, July 26, 2019, <https://news.gallup.com/poll/261680/americans-believe-creationism.aspx>, accessed on 3/18/20.

[23] Sam Allberry, *Is God Anti-Gay?* The Good Book Company, UK, 2015.

[24] John P. Dehlin, "Why People Leave the LDS Church," <https://www.youtube.com/watch?v=uZQJc5SxnVs>, accessed on 3/23/20.

[25] Nicole Blanchard, "Boise Man Set a Ludicrous Goal: Fish 365 Days in 2018," Idaho Statesman, March 5, 2019, <https://www.idahostatesman.com/outdoors/fishing/article226413750.html>, accessed on 3/27/20.

[26] Taken from a sermon by Finny Kuruvilla, Crosspointe Mennonite Church, Baltic, OH, May 30, 2017.

About the Author

Gary Miller was raised in California and today lives with his wife Patty and family in the Pacific Northwest. Gary works with the poor in developing countries and directs the SALT Microfinance Solutions program for Christian Aid Ministries. This program offers business and spiritual teaching to those living in chronic poverty, provides small loans, sets up local village savings groups, and assists them in learning how to use their God-given resources to become sustainable.

Gary has authored the Kingdom-Focused Living series, microfinance manuals, and several booklets for outreach purposes.

Have you been inspired by Gary's materials? Maybe you have questions, or perhaps you even disagree with the author. Share your thoughts by sending an email to kingdomfinance@camoh.org or writing to Christian Aid Ministries, P.O. Box 360, Berlin, Ohio 44610.

About Christian Aid Ministries

C hristian Aid Ministries was founded in 1981 as a nonprofit, tax-exempt 501(c)(3) organization. Its primary purpose is to provide a trustworthy and efficient channel for Amish, Mennonite, and other conservative Anabaptist groups and individuals to minister to physical and spiritual needs around the world. This is in response to the command to ". . . do good unto all men, especially unto them who are of the household of faith" (Galatians 6:10).

Each year, CAM supporters provide 15-20 million pounds of food, clothing, medicines, seeds, Bibles, Bible story books, and other Christian literature for needy people. Most of the aid goes to orphans and Christian families. Supporters' funds also help to clean up and rebuild for natural disaster victims, put up Gospel billboards in the

U.S., support several church-planting efforts, operate two medical clinics, and provide resources for needy families to make their own living. CAM's main purposes for providing aid are to help and encourage God's people and bring the Gospel to a lost and dying world.

CAM has staff, warehouses, and distribution networks in Romania, Moldova, Ukraine, Haiti, Nicaragua, Liberia, Israel, and Kenya. Aside from management, supervisory personnel, and bookkeeping operations, volunteers do most of the work at CAM locations. Each year, volunteers at our warehouses, field bases, Disaster Response Services projects, and other locations donate over 200,000 hours of work.

CAM's ultimate purpose is to glorify God and help enlarge His kingdom. ". . . whatsoever ye do, do all to the glory of God" (1 Corinthians 10:31).

The Way to God and Peace

We live in a world contaminated by sin. Sin is anything that goes against God's holy standards. When we do not follow the guidelines that God our Creator gave us, we are guilty of sin. Sin separates us from God, the source of life.

Since the time when the first man and woman, Adam and Eve, sinned in the Garden of Eden, sin has been universal. The Bible says that we all have "sinned and come short of the glory of God" (Romans 3:23). It also says that the natural consequence for that sin is eternal death, or punishment in an eternal hell: "Then when lust hath conceived, it bringeth forth sin: and sin, when it is finished, bringeth forth death" (James 1:15).

But we do not have to suffer eternal death in hell. God provided forgiveness for our sins through the death of His only Son, Jesus Christ. Because Jesus was perfect and without sin, He could die in our place. "For God so loved the world that he gave his only begotten Son, that whosoever believeth in him should not perish, but have everlasting life" (John 3:16).

A sacrifice is something given to benefit someone else. It costs the giver greatly. Jesus was God's sacrifice. Jesus' death takes away the penalty of sin for all those who accept this sacrifice and truly repent of their sins. To repent of sins means to be truly sorry for and turn away from the things we have done that have violated God's standards (Acts 2:38; 3:19).

Jesus died, but He did not remain dead. After three days, God's Spirit miraculously raised Him to life again. God's Spirit does something similar in us. When we receive Jesus as our sacrifice and repent of our sins, our hearts are changed. We become spiritually alive! We develop new desires and attitudes (2 Corinthians 5:17). We begin to make choices that please God (1 John 3:9). If we do fail and commit sins, we can ask God for forgiveness. "If we confess our sins, he is faithful and just to forgive us our sins, and to cleanse us from all unrighteousness" (1 John 1:9).

Once our hearts have been changed, we want to continue growing spiritually. We will be happy to let Jesus be the Master of our lives and will want to become more like Him. To do this, we must meditate on God's Word and commune with God in prayer. We will testify to others of this change by being baptized and sharing the good news of God's victory over sin and death. Fellowship with a faithful group of believers will strengthen our walk with God (1 John 1:7).